THE CHRISTIAN

idea book

Hundreds of Ideas, Tips, and Activities
to Help You Be a Great Mom

Ellen Banks Elwell

CROSSWAY BOOKS
WHEATON, ILLINOIS

The Christian Mom's Idea Book: Hundreds of Ideas, Tips, and Activities to Help You Be a Great Mom

Copyright © 1997, 2008 by Ellen Banks Elwell

Published by Crossway Books
    a publishing ministry of Good News Publishers
    1300 Crescent Street
    Wheaton, Illinois 60187

Revised edition published in 2008 by Crossway Books

Interior design and typesetting by Lakeside Design Plus
Cover design: Amy Bristow
Cover photo: Getty Images

First printing, 1997, revised edition 2008
Printed in the United States of America

ISBN13 978-1-58134-950-4
ISBN 1-58134-950-5

Unless otherwise indicated, Scripture quotations are from *The Living Bible*, © 1971. Used by permission of Tyndale House Publishers, Inc., Wheaton, IL 60189. All rights reserved.

Scripture references marked NIV are from *The Holy Bible: New International Version®*. Copyright © 1973, 1978, 1984 by International Bible Society. Used by permission of Zondervan Publishing House. All rights reserved.

The "NIV" and "New International Version" trademarks are registered in the United States Patent and Trademark Office by International Bible Society. Use of either trademark requires the permission of International Bible Society.

Library of Congress Cataloging-in-Publication Data
Elwell, Ellen Banks, 1952–
    The Christian mom's idea book : hundreds of ideas, tips, and activities to help you be a great mom / Ellen Banks Elwell.—Rev. ed.
        p. cm.
    Includes bibliographical references.
    ISBN 978-1-58134-950-4 (tpb)
    1. Mothers—Life skill guides. 2. Mothers—Religious life. 3. Motherhood—Religious aspects—Christianity. I. Title.
HQ759.E47 2008
248.8'431—dc22

                                      2007049265

VP	16	15	14	13	12	11	10	09	08
	9	8	7	6	5	4	3	2	1

Contents

Contents

Preface

Motherhood is a fascinating subject to me—probably because I am the grateful mom of Chad, Nate (and Brit), and Jordan. They have brought great joy into my life, and I continue to learn from each of them.

When I was a young mother, I watched other moms closely, choosing to implement for myself the ideas and ways of relating that I valued and respected. I'm still extremely interested in how other moms think, plan, and relate to their children. What works for them? What might work for me? What can we learn from one another?

In the movie *Shadowlands*, one of C. S. Lewis's students remarked, "We read to know we're not alone." I strongly identify with this statement. I'm grateful for authors who have enriched my life, more than they'll ever know, by allowing me windows into their experience. I remember various times in early motherhood that were particularly lonely and overwhelming. Some of the books I read helped me realize that I wasn't the only mom with such feelings, and I was encouraged to take a more honest approach toward myself, God, and others.

This book of ideas, stories, suggestions, and interviews has been gathered from over eighty moms I admire—sharp ladies with children living at home who have positive attitudes, show respect for others, and enjoy learning. I have included many ideas from many moms, in their own words, realizing that no mother can possibly incorporate all of them into her life, but hoping you will find some to enrich yours. While compiling this material, I've had great fun trying out some of the ideas myself. I should have started this project nineteen years ago, *before* I had kids!

It is my hope and prayer that the contents of this book will be insightful, helpful, and encouraging. May your connections with the hearts and homes of other moms represented in this book be helpful to each of you in your particular stage of motherhood.

Acknowledgments

This book is dedicated to the eighty-two moms who gave me more than 500 great ideas.

Faith Aagaard, Carol Ahrenholz, Jean Allen, Carol Balow, Alice Banks, Carolyn Barron, Karen Beardsley, Sue Bedrossian, Lynne Bensinger, Christy Bollier, Sue Boutwell, Terri Bradford, Sarah Bradley, Janet Burgess, Beth Chase, Joyce Clouse, Cindy Clousing, Julie Clum, Kathi Couture, Marty Daily, Joan Darnauer, Joanne DeGroot, Amy Dennis, Carlene Ellerman, Joyce Fletcher, Ruth Gibson, Mary Gieser, Denise Gill, Rose Graham, Kathy Green, Deborah Grobe, Cynthie Haag, Nancy Hensley, Kita Heslinga, Debbie Hollinger, Linda Hoisington, Ruthie Howard, Linnea Hubbell, Marti Huitsing, Sharon Irvin, Susan Jahns, Janet Jarvis, Joan Johnson, Phebe Johnson, Sheila Johnson, Sharon Kettinger, Barbara Korell, Linda Ladd, Beth Larson, Ann Lawrenz, Nancy Leach, Nancy Lewis, Shelley Madeira, Lori Maillefer, Beth Mansy, Shirley Mathews, Linda McCormick, Brenda Rowell McDonell, Kathy Murray, Marsha Nygren, Juli Painter, Nancy Paist, Carole Paulsen, Gail Pflederer, Linda Pinckney, Jennifer Richardson, Jeanne Rodenkirch, Jennifer Rownd, Mary Ryken, Becky Sandberg, Ruthie Schroeder, Dawn Scott, Debbie Seward, Linda Bright Simmons, Kathy Stefo, Joan Stough, Bev Swanson, Carol Taylor, Jan Teat, Lilla Toelcke, Cheryl Anne Waterman, Jennifer Wheatley.

I offer special thanks to Denise Gill, Sharon Irvin, Linda McCormick, and Gail Pflederer for reading the manuscript and giving me helpful advice and encouragement.

Introduction

Are you the perfect mother? I'm not. Do you wish you *could* be? Don't we all! I know I can never be a perfect mom, but because God gives wisdom when I seek it and instruction from His Word, I want to continue to learn and grow.

In this day when tolerance for any and all opinions is encouraged, I'm grateful for the Bible, my plumb line of truth. When wallpapering a room, hanging a plumb line on the wall is the first thing I do. Made by suspending a weight from a string, the plumb line provides an accurate vertical line. I don't depend on my eyes; relying on the law of gravity is much safer. After marking the first straight line on the wall, I continue lining one piece against the last, hoping I'll come out with attractive results at the end. Now, I didn't say the results would be *perfect*. Whenever my husband and I wallpaper together, about the eighth time that I comment, "Oh, no one will ever notice that," we look at each other and smile. Never perfect, we have nevertheless ended up with some good-looking wallpaper jobs. Motherhood is like that. If I approach it according to God's plan, there can be attractive results.

Making a cameo appearance at the end of Proverbs is a woman who is an excellent mother from a biblical perspective. The wife and mother described in this passage is quite a lady! She is not passive, fearful, helpless, or uninformed. On the contrary, she is described as being industrious, compassionate, wise, secure, loyal to her husband, blessed by her children—and the list goes on. It's interesting that the book of Proverbs begins and ends with women who are on a good track. The woman at the beginning represents wisdom, and the woman at the end is a portrait of a wise wife and mother. In between, however, we run into some women who are clearly on the wrong track.

It is better to live in the corner of an attic than
with a crabby woman in a lovely home.
PROVERBS 21:9

A beautiful woman lacking discretion and modesty
is like a fine gold ring in a pig's snout.
PROVERBS 11:22

A wise woman builds her house, while a foolish
woman tears hers down by her own efforts.
PROVERBS 14:1

Proverbs 31 opens with warnings to King Lemuel from his mother. She is anxious for him to avoid things that would trip him up and destroy his leadership. In the original Hebrew language, verses 10–31 were written as an acrostic (a poetic form that suggests a complete exploration of the subject at hand). Describing a rare and valuable wife and mother, the passage consists of twenty-two couplets, each beginning with a letter of the Hebrew alphabet. Following along with that idea, I have compiled an acrostic on the word Motherhood, summarizing the characteristics of the wife and mother described in Proverbs 31:10–31, shared in the next chapter.

Part One

Connecting with the Bible

I once heard a story about four pastors who were discussing their favorite translations of the Bible. One liked the King James Version, *and another liked the* New American Standard Bible. *Yet another liked* The New Living Translation. *When the conversation came around to the fourth pastor, he said that he liked his mother's translation the best. Acting surprised, the other three men said they hadn't realized his mother had translated the Bible. "Oh yes," he responded. "She translated the Bible into life, and it was the most convincing translation I ever saw."*

John Wesley is reported as saying, "I learnt more about God through my mother than through all the theologians of England."

Each day we mothers sow seeds in our children's lives. These seeds can be for good or for ill. When we go to the Bible, we are provided with seed that has an eternal shelf life. The picture of motherhood found there inspires and equips us for our task today!

1

An Acrostic on Motherhood

Merciful

The virtuous woman showed compassion and kindness to her family, but also to others around her. Proverbs 31 reveals that the hard-working woman of excellence was prosperous both spiritually and physically. But in her success she didn't shrink back from helping others. The same hands that were busy being successful reached out to benefit others.

> A woman made unfeeling by wealth is a monster. If she is so busy holding the distaff (spindle) or the pen that she becomes hard and insensitive to the cry of misery, she has lost her glory.[1]

When we mothers reach out to people outside our families, our own families receive a sense of security as a result of our deeds. Of course, this will be reassuring to our families only if we are first of all meeting their needs. If we're not, the family will understandably resent our gestures to others.

> She sews for the poor, and generously gives to the needy.
> VERSES 19–20,

I used to think of "poor" as meaning destitute or penniless, and it can mean that. But the broader meaning of "poor," and especially of "needy," is to lack or need something. My friend who just had surgery lacks energy. I can take her a meal or offer to vacuum her home. The neighbor whose husband lost his job appreciates phone calls, encouragement, and prayer. My friend who is experiencing depression needs my time and a listening ear. Having been the needy person before, I treasure in my heart the acts of love and kindness that were shown to me by my family and friends. They truly became the arms of Christ around me. The poor do not dwell only in the inner city or third-world countries. They are all around me, if I have the eyes to see their situation and ears to hear their cries for help.

> God blesses those who are kind to the poor.
> He helps them out of their troubles.
> PSALM 41:1

Observant

> She watches carefully all that goes on
> throughout her household.
> VERSE 27

Watching over the household is one of the most important parts of a mother's job description. Listening is right up there with watching. This mom was observant, and she was also perceptive. Observing means seeing what is going on; perceiving is going a step further and understanding.

We observe in so many ways. Think back to the first night your first baby slept at home. You probably *watched*. I wasn't quite sure what I was looking for, but I observed intensely. Even though our new baby slept right next to our bed that first night, I kept waking up and checking him. As our children grow, we continue to monitor their physical health and safety. We keep an eye on their choices of friends and try to encourage them in good directions. We look out for their spiritual growth, their educational progress, and their emotional wholeness.

If your children are school-age, you'll understand how I can immediately pick up on what kind of day my children have had by watching the way they walk in the door and by listening to their tone of voice. Two examples come to mind.

Our sixteen-year-old son, Chad, had been dating a girl for some months. He's a pretty even-keeled personality, so when I noticed that he seemed a little glum one week, I wondered why. (I watch my children for the big patterns; isolated ups and downs will come and go, especially during the adolescent years.) One morning when I dropped him off at school, I knew that my husband, Jim, would be away for the evening, so I asked Chad if he'd like to go out for dinner together—he could choose the place. He accepted. That night, over dinner, he started talking. I don't know about teenage girls, but if you feed guys, they talk. When Chad explained that he and the girl he had been dating had decided not to be "an item" anymore, I better understood his behavior for the previous week. I listened a lot and asked a few questions. As we left the restaurant, I felt proud of him for having wrestled through some important issues, and I was thankful that I had been watching.

Years ago our son, Nate, then in junior high, tried out for his school's basketball team. He made the first few cuts and came up to the last day—the finals. Watching him come out of the gym door that afternoon, I could immediately tell by the way he walked to the car that he had not made the team. How disappointed he was! Displaying maturity in the way he handled the news, he didn't put down the coach or the other boys who made the team. But I was a little surprised when he started saying things like, "Well, I really didn't want to be on the team anyway." I wasn't sure that he was being honest with himself, so I watched and listened. His sadness needed to come out eventually, I thought. Sure enough, it did.

That night before he went to sleep, I went into his room and sat on the edge of his bed. All I had to do was ask a few questions about how he was feeling, and the tears began to flow. It was a healthy release. For a while I didn't say much; I just rubbed his back. Then I told him that I appreciated the honesty of his feelings, and I shed some tears with him. Grieving is an important part of any loss—no matter what stage of life we're at. We prayed together that God would fill that empty spot with something else. The remarkable ending to this story is that after a few weeks, one of the boys on the team didn't qualify because of grades, and Nathan was invited on in his place. There was a lot of happiness in the house *that* night. (There was also a rather expensive trip to the store to purchase new basketball shoes, but it was worth it!)

As my sons were growing up, I sometimes grew weary and complained about the many hours I spent driving them to music lessons, school events, and sports events, etc. In my better moments, though, I tried to remember that motherhood is a privilege. Moms are blessed with the responsibility to plan for and observe the well-being of future leaders!

Trustworthy

Her husband can trust her,
and she will richly satisfy his needs.
VERSE 11

To trust is to rely firmly on the integrity and character of another person. I like Charles Swindoll's explanation of integrity: "the distance between life and lip." Do my husband and kids see a distance between what I say and how I act? Can my husband have confidence in my ability to manage the household?

When our children see trust modeled in their parents' marriage, they have a great foundation for personal security. The child reasons, "If Dad trusts Mom and treats her with respect, he'll treat me that way too. If Mom trusts Dad and treats him with respect, she'll treat me that way too." On the contrary, if children see Mommy intimating that "Daddy is a dummy" or hear Daddy suggest that "Mommy is an ogre" (or vice versa), they are quick to realize that their parents don't have a united front, allowing for weak spots (more like gaping holes!) in the protective walls of the home.[2]

> I have seen what uncertainty and mistrust do to people. When they cannot count on the systems of their community, when they see that the general motive of the world is selfishness, and when they suspect that nothing *has* to be what it says it is, that anyone might be deceiving them, (1) they fear the world, as though they were strangers in a strange land, and feel helpless. Or (2) they fight back; they themselves become selfish and uncaring on the premise that all existence is "dog eat dog." In either case, the security of a trustworthy *home* could have protected them, strengthened them, and kept them virtuous in spite of the instability outside. People need to experience trust in order themselves to be confident and truthful. The dependable marriage is a fortress—not to keep them from the world, but to steady them, to strengthen them for entering into that world.[3]

I discovered that the Hebrew word used to describe the trust of this woman's husband is the same word used in Psalm 25:3—"None who have faith in God will ever be disgraced for trusting him."

> The bond uniting husband and wife in a true marriage is not unlike that uniting us with God. Happy are they who by their trust in one another and the peaceful joys which it brings are led to united trust in a yet deeper love, mirrored to them in their own![4]

If a husband can trust in the character, conduct, and speech of his wife, he is greatly blessed, and so are her kids.

Helpful

She will not hinder him, but help him all her life.
VERSE 12

The possibilities here are endless. I can be helpful to my husband physically, emotionally, spiritually, and mentally. Listening and asking questions is a great place to start. What is he feeling and thinking? What's going on at work? Is something overwhelming? Maybe there's something I can do to help lighten the load. We might need an evening out for coffee, or maybe he needs a ten-minute nap after dinner. "The best relationships are built up, like a fine lacquer finish, with accumulated layers of acts of kindness" (Alan McGinnis).

The opposite of building up is tearing down, and unfortunately it is not difficult to fall into destructive patterns.

A worthy wife is her husband's joy and crown; the other kind
corrodes his strength and tears down everything he does.
PROVERBS 12:4

A wise woman builds her house, while a foolish
woman tears hers down by her own efforts.
PROVERBS 14:1

Have you ever come away from time spent with another couple having observed sarcasm (anger in disguise), put-downs, or mockery from one spouse to the other? How sad and how painful. That's an example of tearing the house down by one's own efforts.

In the creation account, God said that since it wasn't good for man to be alone, He would make a companion for him, a *helper*.

The fact that a spouse is termed a "helper" declares that marriage was never an end in itself, but a preparation. We've accomplished no great thing, yet, in getting married. We have not *completed* a relationship (though many a fool assumes that the hard work's been done with the wedding and turns attention to other interests). Rather, we've established the terms by which we will now go to work. And it's in this "helping" one another that, ideally, we will grow more and more to be one. . . . When we love each other—when we are a help unto the other, in likeness and in unlikeness—then we are in fact also loving God, whose ordinance we are obeying.[5]

It's the small choices we make each day that accumulate in order to end up with the beautiful finish we all desire.

Energetic

She is energetic, a hard worker.
VERSE 17

The Proverbs 31 mother displayed vigorous activity. She found wool and flax and spun them. She bought imported foods. She got up early to prepare breakfast. She planted a vineyard. And the list goes on. (I get tired just reading the chapter!) Some mothers seem to have more of this commodity than others, but I believe energy has more to do with choices than we sometimes realize. When my schedule is under control, when I'm exercising regularly, when I'm digesting the truth of the Bible, and when I'm watching how I'm thinking, I feel more energized. Hindrances to energy include wrong attitudes, overcommitment, and poor physical condition. Each of us experiences times when energy is low—after childbirth, during an illness, when there's been a loss. But when we look at the overall patterns of our life, if a consistent lack of energy is a problem, we may need to look closely at choices we're making in order to discover and attain increased vigor.

Our example of excellence showed diligence in her sphere of influence first within her home and then within the community. The majority of a mom's work is done alone and in humble situations—doing laundry, making meals, cleaning up messes, running errands. When my children were very young, I remember wishing that someone could be around to applaud me for doing all the small, motherly tasks throughout the day. Actually, Someone was.

> Whatever you do, work at it with all your heart, as
> working for the Lord, not for men, since you know
> that you will receive an inheritance from the Lord as
> a reward. It is the Lord Christ you are serving.
> COLOSSIANS 3:23–24, NIV

Besides making good choices, I also must know where to go to get the energy and stamina I need to do the job.

> Don't you yet understand? Don't you know by now
> that the everlasting God, the Creator of the farthest parts of
> the earth, never grows faint or weary?
> No one can fathom the depths of his understanding. He
> gives power to the tired and worn out,
> and strength to the weak. Even the youths
> shall be exhausted, and the young men will all give up.
> But they that wait upon the Lord shall renew their strength.
> They shall mount up with wings like eagles;
> they shall run and not be weary; they
> shall walk and not faint.
> ISAIAH 40:28–31

When I think of energetic women, I think of my mother, Betty Banks. Now in her seventies, she's still on the move. Several years ago she and my dad hired a gentleman to paint the outside of their house. After one week of watching her come and go, the painter said, "Your energy is incredible! If I'm ever in the hospital needing a blood transfusion, can I ask for some of *your* blood?"

Reverent Toward God

Charm can be deceptive and beauty doesn't
last, but a woman who fears and reverences
God shall be greatly praised.
VERSE 30

There's certainly a contrast here between what's temporary and what's lasting. Reverence for God is at the very foundation of this woman's excellent life. Everything she is and everything she does is guided by her respect for God.

> Beauty recommends none to God, but it has deceived many a man who has made his choice of a wife by it. It is a fading thing at best. A fit of sickness will stain and sully it in a little time; a thousand accidents may blast this flower in its prime, old age will certainly wither it and death and the grave consume it. But the fear of God reigning in the heart is the beauty of the soul; it recommends those that have it to the favour of God, and is, in His sight, of great price; it will last forever, and bid defiance to death itself, which consumes the beauty of the body, but consummates the beauty of the soul.[6]

How do we develop the inner beauty of a soul that reverences God? Mary, the mother of Jesus, shines as a great example. In her Magnificat, recorded in Luke 1:46–55, Mary first praised God (vv. 46–48). Second, she acknowledged her humble state (vv. 48–49). Third, she built her life on God's plan—she obeyed.

Think about it. God wasn't sending Jesus to be born and raised by an experienced mother. Mary had *no* experience. God sent His only Son into arms that were young and fragile. But Mary had something else, something that was highly valued by God. Mary had reverence—reverence that produced obedience.

The benefits of reverence for God are the same now as they were generations ago:

- *Wisdom.* "Where is the man who fears the Lord? God will teach him how to choose the best" (Ps. 25:12).
- *Friendship with God.* "Friendship with God is reserved for those who reverence him. With them alone he shares the secrets of his promises" (Ps. 25:14).
- *Mercy.* "He is like a father to us, tender and sympathetic to those who reverence him" (Ps. 103:13).
- *Help and protection.* "All of you, his people, trust in him. He is your helper; he is your shield" (Ps. 115:11).

Honored

Her children stand and bless her; so does her husband.
VERSE 28

Don't we all like to be honored? Don't we all like to see our children recognized, or to be recognized by them? I appreciate encouraging words from people of all ages, but there's some-

Things I Really Like about My Mom

Grade 2: She gives me atenchen (attention).

Grade 3: She lets the cat sleep in my room.

Grade 4: She loves God.

Grade 5: She almost never looks weird on Saturdays.

Grade 6: My mom loves me and will never stop loving me.

Grade 7: She always comes to watch me play sports.

Grade 8: She doesn't lecture me.

Grade 9: She tries to be the best mother she can be. It's hard, because we don't make it easy.

Grade 10: She's a great cook.

Grade 11: My mom respects my dad. She's teaching me how to be a good wife by the way she relates to my dad.

Grade 12: She's giving me increasing freedom with age.

Things I Wish My Mom Would Do Differently

Grade 2: I wish she wouldn't talk on the phone so much.

Grade 3: I wish she would let us see her wedding dress.

Grade 4: I wish she'd let me quit piano. I hate piano!

Grade 5: I wish she wouldn't follow a stupid health book that doesn't work a single bit!

Grade 6: I wish she wouldn't pack so much luggage when we go on trips; everybody stares at us!

Grade 7: I wish she didn't put mushrooms in everything.

Grade 8: I wish she wouldn't tell me over and over how disorganized I am. Once is enough!

Grade 9: I wish she'd go easy on the "When I was your age . . ." speech.

Grade 10: I wish she wouldn't show such outward favoritism to my siblings.

Grade 11: I wish her supersonic hearing would go away. She always complains that my music is too loud, even when the door to my room is shut and I can barely hear it. She can even hear my dad blink!

Grade 12: I wish she would make fewer sweeping statements.

thing truly special about the honor I receive from my kids. Not only am I honored by their kind words and gestures but also by their lives.

I'll never forget the night Jordan (five at the time) told me he thought I was "loveful, beautiful, and heartful." Another never-to-be-forgotten moment happened on the day of my grandmother's funeral. Living to be 103, she was dearly loved by the whole family. At one point in the service I was getting rather teary, and Nathan (then ten) leaned over and put his arm around me, keeping it there for the rest of the service. I'll never forget that gesture as long as I live. Also etched in my memory is the Friday afternoon that Chad (seventeen at the time) was chosen by his high school student body as Homecoming King. Hearing his name announced at the pep assembly, I alternated between crying and wanting to go ballistic! Jim and I were elated that Chad had been honored, and we also felt honored because we were his parents.

Even though I like receiving affirmation *from* my kids, I cannot live *for* their affirmation. The Bible clearly teaches that we parents aren't here to accommodate our children, but rather to love them, lead them, and teach them. They are constantly watching the quality of our lives.

There are some things my kids and I agree on all the time; there are other things we agree on only some of the time; and yes, there are a few things we never seem to agree on. That's okay. Our boys are encouraged to discuss with us anything that doesn't seem fair to them, and we're willing to take a second look. Some issues, they understand, are non-negotiable. But others are not "hills to die on," and we try to be as reasonable as possible. When we're not, we apologize. Kids don't lose respect when we make mistakes but apologize. They do lose respect for us as parents when we deny or rationalize our mistakes.

A challenge out of James Dobson's book *Dare to Discipline* hits me right between the eyes each time I read it:

> If Christian parents are perceived by a child as not being worthy of respect, then neither is their religion, or their morals, or their government, or their country, or any of their values. This becomes the generation gap at its most basic level.[7]

How are we doing? Are we living lives before God that are worthy of our children's respect?

> I will try to walk a blameless path, but how I need your help, especially in my own home, where I long to act as I should.
> PSALM 101:2

Orator of Wisdom

When she speaks, her words are wise,
and kindness is the rule for everything she says.
VERSE 26

It's curious that the morning I worked on this part of the acrostic was a morning that I didn't do so hot in this area. As my two oldest children were getting ready to leave for school, my words were characterized more as impatient than kind and wise. I'm thankful that God, through His Word:

- *Catches me up short.* He shows me my sin, but I'm not left despairing. "The whole Bible was given to us by inspiration from God and is useful to teach us what is true and to make us realize what is wrong in our lives; it straightens us out and helps us do what is right" (2 Tim. 3:16).
- *Reminds me of His grace.* "But if we confess our sins to him, he can be depended on to forgive us and to cleanse us from every wrong" (1 John 1:9).
- *Encourages me toward good choices.* "But make everyone rejoice who puts his trust in you. Keep them shouting for joy because you are defending them. Fill all who love you with your happiness. For you bless the godly man, O Lord; you protect him with your shield of love" (Ps. 5:11–12).

What a host of choices we make in our speech every day—in our early-morning words, our getting-ready words, our telephone words, our reminder words, our mealtime words, our bedtime words. The actual words, the tone of voice we use, and the timing are all significant in communicating to those around us.

Not only does the woman of excellence run an orderly *house*, but she has an orderly *heart*, which flows into orderly *speech*. "The law of love and kindness is written in the heart, but it shows itself in the tongue."[8] Like most issues in our lives, it all goes back to our hearts.

Wisdom and *kindness.* The two words sound beautiful, don't they? Both words are mentioned many times throughout the book of Proverbs. Listed below are some of these verses. I have written these on individual 3 x 5 cards, and I like referring to them often.

A wise man holds his tongue. Only a fool blurts out
everything he knows; that only leads to sorrow and trouble.
PROVERBS 10:14

The upright speak what is helpful;
the wicked speak rebellion.
PROVERBS 10:32

Evil words destroy. Godly skill rebuilds.
PROVERBS 11:9

A gossip goes around spreading rumors,
while a trustworthy man tries to quiet them.
PROVERBS 11:13

Your own soul is nourished when you are kind;
it is destroyed when you are cruel.
PROVERBS 11:17

Gentle words cause life and health;
griping brings discouragement.
PROVERBS 15:4

Kind words are like honey—
enjoyable and healthful.
PROVERBS 16:24

Never forget to be truthful and kind.
Hold these virtues tightly.
Write them deep within your heart.
PROVERBS 3:3

If we moms want to unlock the door to wisdom in our speech, here is the key:

Yes, if you want better insight and discernment, and are searching for them as you would for lost money or hidden treasure, then wisdom will be given you, and knowledge of God himself; you will soon learn the importance of reverence for the Lord and of trusting him. For the Lord grants wisdom! His every word is a treasure of knowledge and understanding. He grants good sense to the godly—his saints. He is their shield, protecting them and guarding their pathway. He shows how to distinguish right from wrong, how to find the right decision every time. For wisdom and truth will enter the very center of your being, filling your life with joy.

PROVERBS 2:3–10

Of Noble Character

A wife of noble character
who can find?
VERSE 10, NIV

A noble woman exhibits the qualities of courage and generosity.

Courage means facing fear with confidence. As one person said, "Courage in people is like a tea bag. You never know their strength until they're in hot water." The opposite of courage is fear, a powerful emotion. In a crisis situation, fear gets the adrenaline rushing in our bodies, and we are mobilized for action. It can be helpful! But fear as a constant companion is highly destructive. Fear stops our success and inhibits our productivity. When we're fearful, we worry. The word *worry* comes from an old Anglo-Saxon word that means "to strangle." According to Corrie ten Boom, "Worry does not empty tomorrow of its sorrow—it empties today of its strength." If fear surrounds us, security is gone, because fear and security cannot coexist. When I struggle with fear, which I do more than I'd like to admit, I refer to reassuring Scriptures such as:

My protection and success come from God alone.
He is my refuge, a Rock where no enemy can reach
me. O my people, trust him all the time. Pour out
your longings before him, for he can help!
PSALM 62:7–8

For God did not give us a spirit of timidity, but a
spirit of power, of love and of self-discipline.
2 TIMOTHY 1:7, NIV

Don't worry about anything; instead, pray about everything;
tell God your needs and don't forget to thank him for his
answers. If you do this you will experience God's peace,
which is far more wonderful than the human mind can
understand. His peace will keep your thoughts and your
hearts quiet and at rest as you trust in Christ Jesus.
PHILIPPIANS 4:6–7

Regarding *generosity*, the virtuous woman was liberal with
her giving in many ways—to her own family first and then to
others. My parents have always been generous people. I have
experienced and appreciated this because I have been a recipient and also because I have seen their generosity extended to
more people and families than I can count. They have shown
special time and attention to widows, the disabled, their own
parents in old age, missionaries, etc. I am grateful for their
example.

I also have friends whose lives are marked by generosity.
My friend Phebe helps keep a local bread company in business, buying freshly baked loaves of bread for her friends and
dropping them off every few weeks. Another friend and her
husband built a new home several years ago. They included
two guest rooms, complete with bathrooms, kitchenettes, and
a laundry area that they make available to various people who
need a place to stay for a short while. These friends are a great
inspiration to me! It's heartwarming to see people using God's
resources for such acts of kindness.

Dignified

She is a woman of strength and dignity,
and has no fear of old age.
VERSE 25

According to the *American Heritage Dictionary*, *dignity* is the state of being worthy of respect.

> The capable woman wins the respect and honour of her husband and children and those of the wider community, not least because her own commitment to God underlies this productive life of hers.[9]

Before we can accept respect from others, we must be able to respect ourselves. As a new bride struggling with questions about my role as an adult woman, I read the book *Ms. Means Myself* by Gladys Hunt. It is a book I have returned to over and over again. Many years after I first read it, I'm still appreciating some of her thoughts. For example:

> We have freedom of knowing that our personal worth is bound up in God's character. Because of God's initiative in redemption, I'm free to accept myself because God has accepted me—and I can follow God's example in reaching out with love to others. I can also be free to forgive, because I am forgiven. . . . We make our own prisons. God's invitation is to come out.[10]

God gives us many invitations throughout Holy Scripture. One offered to the children of Israel many years ago is also His offer to you and me today:

> "For I am the Lord your God who brought you
> out of the land of Egypt, with the intention that
> you be slaves no longer; I have broken your
> chains and will make you walk with dignity."
> LEVITICUS 26:13

How hopeful this is for all of us! We don't have to live fearful, passive lives. We can live lives that are full of freedom, adventure, and dignity!

According to Proverbs 31:10, the woman described in this acrostic is worth far more than jewels. She's hard to put a price tag on, she's worth so much! As we consistently connect with God's wisdom and strength, we will make healthy choices leading to becoming mothers of great value.

Part Two

Connecting with Other Moms

This section of the book can be considered a sort of handbook or directory for moms. Subjects are arranged alphabetically, and the categories have been chosen with busy moms in mind. Consequently, it's not necessary to read them in any particular order, although if you like reading straight through from the front to the back, that's okay.

Most of the sections begin with introductions, which I wrote, followed by ideas from contributing moms (sometimes several run together). Several sections are the results of interviews with moms or professionals whose expertise I sought on particular topics.

Please approach this part of The Christian Mom's Idea Book in the same way you would approach a smorgasbord. Just as we cannot eat every item at a buffet, neither can we attempt (or even think of attempting) every idea in the following sections. Also, this book is not intended to make a mom feel guilty; it's meant to be a helpful resource. So if each mom reading through these categories comes away with five or ten ideas she finds helpful, this book will accomplish its purpose.

2

Baby-sitters

~~~

Our family was blessed with terrific baby-sitters during our sons' younger years. Chad and Nathan still remember one Saturday afternoon when Jenny baby-sat, and the three of them become locked *inside* our smallest bedroom for three hours. Unable to get the lock to work and not having a telephone, Jenny made the best of a bad situation, and all three of them were happy when we arrived home. (I paid her extremely well that day.) The boys also remember funny stories that Julie used to make up and tell to them before they went to bed. Julie's probably still making up interesting stories for the fifth grade class that she teaches today! It makes me feel old to think that Jenny now has three sons of her own, and Julie is married.

Whenever Jim and I needed a baby-sitter for the kids, I was very particular about who I asked. I wanted a responsible teenager or college student who would treat the boys with respect, and expect their respect as well. At the top of our list were baby-sitters who could handle an emergency, if one arose, and be creative enough to entertain the kids through reading, story-telling, or game playing. If I couldn't find a baby-sitter whom I trusted or felt comfortable with, we didn't go out. After all, children are more important than schedules.

Ideas from Other Moms

● When my children have been struggling with separation anxiety, I have found it helpful to leave a little present (Lifesavers, a Matchbox car, etc.) with the baby-sitter. I make sure that the child knows he can have it only if he doesn't make a scene when we leave the house. This has worked wonders for us.

● We have tried to invite selected baby-sitters over a few days beforehand for a meal or an ice cream treat. It's been fun to get to know the sitters better ourselves, and the kids really look forward to time alone with them when we have to be gone.

● I like to make the baby-sitting of our children as pleasant an experience as possible, so that our baby-sitters want to keep coming back. I try to have the house in order and to stock their favorite beverage. I often prepare a homemade snack for them and leave it out on the counter. In order to help them feel comfortable in *any* circumstance or emergency, I always fill out a form that includes the phone numbers of several neighbors, our family doctor, and a local relative. It is also important to write down our address and phone number, just in case they're needed and the sitter can't quite come up with the information. I also have a form filled out on each child that lists vital information about them, including insurance policy info, so that if they become seriously injured, precious time will not be wasted.

● Our teenage daughter does so much baby-sitting that she records all of her jobs on a calendar. We have also been encouraging her to record the amount she is paid for each job. *Tip*: I wish all parents paid their sitters by check. It helps teenagers learn banking skills and promotes saving. It is just too easy for teens to spend cash and have little accounting for it.

● Regularly used baby-sitters are *great*. They become like family to our children. A history of games, expectations, respect, and love between the child and the sitter develops. On the days that I work, my children go to their friends' houses (women who are in my Sunday school class who also have children). Having children the same age to play with at their own house also creates a fun atmosphere for my children.

3

The Bible

May I never forget your words; for they are my only hope.
Therefore I will keep obeying you forever and forever,
free within the limits of your laws.
PSALM 119:43–45

One spring break I was sitting in a chair on a Florida beach watching Jim and Jordan fly one of my dad's heavy-duty kites. The deep red kite against the aqua blue sky was gorgeous. Just as a kite is designed to be flown in the wind at the end of a long string, so we are designed by God our Maker to fly and soar as we live by His guidelines, recorded in the Bible. We and the kite both get into trouble when our strings are tangled or cut. Thankfully, our Maker knows us well and is merciful and patient, helping us untangle and reconnect, getting our kites back up and into the wind. One of the mysteries of our Christian experience is that *we can only experience true freedom within the limits of God's laws.*

Ideas from Other Moms

Moms and the Bible

- The Bible has helped me to be a better mom (and wife, daughter, sister, friend). At times I struggle with worry, impatience, discontentment, low self-esteem, weariness, and anger. The Bible offers so much wisdom in all these areas. I still have a long way to go, but the Bible has been my helpful guide during twenty-one years of motherhood.

- For years I was distracted during my Bible reading time in the morning because things that needed to be done during the day kept popping into my head. I decided to keep a pen and notepad next to my Bible. Now when that happens, I write down my thoughts, freeing my mind to concentrate on what I'm reading. Since the "needs" are written down, I can attend to them later.

- I don't read how-to books because they make me feel inadequate, which I already know I am. Without seeming to be trite, I think the Bible has been my greatest help in being a mother. Staying close to the Word and being challenged to be the most Christlike *person* I can be helps me the most in being the best *mother* I can be.

- The Bible keeps me on an even keel emotionally, arms me to face each day, and is packed with wisdom. The Bible has helped me to see how imperfect I am and how much God loves me despite my shortcomings. This has also allowed me to view my imperfect children from God's perspective.

Children and the Bible

- Don't underestimate a young reader's ability to enjoy and understand reading straight from the Bible. Our young reader developed a wonderful habit of crawling in bed at night and reading from her *Living Bible* paraphrase. I'm amazed at the number of books of the Bible she has already

37

read in her comparatively short life. Devotional books are beneficial also, though I especially like to encourage reading from the Bible itself.

● Deuteronomy 11:19 (NIV) tells us, "Teach them [the laws of God] to your children, talking about them when you sit at home and when you walk along the road, when you lie down and when you get up." We try to talk daily about God and frequently verbalize a thankful heart.

● I was trying to encourage Bible memorization with little success until I developed an incentive plan. I took Erik (age five) to a teachers' supply store and let him pick out a variety of five- and ten-cent treasures. Now when he memorizes a verse he receives a treasure from the goody bag.

● We take turns having the children read from a Bible story book after supper. We have also worked at Bible memory as a family. Choosing a chapter or passage that no one has already memorized, we learn it together. It has been great to see the four-year-old rattle off all the verses along with the thirty-nine-year-old. Proverbs 3 is a great chapter to start with.

● One summer before a family vacation, two of our sons, eight and ten, wanted to know how they could earn some spending money. I had been thinking that it would be good to get them reading and memorizing in the book of Proverbs. So I chose twenty-five verses to memorize and typed them out, giving a copy to each son. Sitting down with them and explaining a little about the book of Proverbs, I told them that if they read the whole book and memorized the twenty-five verses, I would give them each an amount they agreed was worth working for. They did this with great excitement!

God appreciates and rewards parents' creativity in helping their children (and themselves) make His Word an intimate part of their lives.

4

Birthday Parties

~~∽◯∽~~

*T*here's nothing like having or attending a birthday party to widen the eyes of a child—such pure excitement! As I was compiling the information for this book, I kept all the suggestions moms gave me in a fat three-ring binder, with labeled dividers for each category of ideas. Shortly after, I took the notebook with me to Phoenix, Arizona, where I attended a convention with my husband. Flying back from Phoenix to Chicago, I sat next to a lovely woman who had just enjoyed a visit with her daughter's family, and her time there included a creative birthday party for her granddaughter.

When she saw me working on birthday party ideas, she got excited, telling me all about her granddaughter's party. It was titled "Under the Sea." The children entered through a submarine (made out of a large refrigerator box). On a huge poster board the parents had drawn a shark, complete with teeth, with an open hole in its mouth big enough to fit a child's head. Each child stood behind the poster and had their picture taken "inside" the shark, using a Polaroid camera. As soon as the pictures were developed, they were hung around the children's necks with yarn. The menu for lunch was sandwiches cut into the shape of fish, Jello with Gummi fish, and a fish cake. Moms come up with such *clever* ideas!

Ideas from Other Moms

● When my girls turned three, I started giving them birthday parties and have continued every year since. I enjoy planning the parties, and they do too. I have saved all their invitations, along with a list of those invited, what we ate, what we did, the birthday girl's reactions, and some pictures. I plan on surprising them by arranging it all in a scrapbook and giving it to them on some special day, the date of which hasn't been decided yet because we are still giving birthday parties!

● The best time of day for birthday parties with young children is morning or midday. Both children and mothers are more pleasant and have more energy then.

● I probably don't do enough special things for my kids, but I do like to make birthdays very special. The parties are not huge and expensive. My goal is to be creative and yet keep the cost as minimal as possible. I choose a theme for the party and limit the number of children invited to the age of the child (seven children for seven years, etc.) until the child is ten years old. Here are some ideas, but keep in mind that I have girls. Guys might need something a little different.

Miss Lovely Lady Party. The girls arrived very dressed up. At the party was a large trunk full of old dresses, hats, furs, purses, etc. The little girls donned their dream outfits, and we made them up with makeup and perfume and painted their nails. We then took a Polaroid photo of them, which they took home.

Backwards Party. An invitation (written backwards) asked guests to dress backwards for the party. Upon arrival, guests were told, "Good-bye. Thanks for the gift!" Cake and ice cream were eaten immediately, and then gifts were opened. Games such as Backwards Basketball and Backwards Relay Races were played. Pizza was eaten at the end of the party, and they were sent home with, "Hi! I'm glad you're here!"

Teddy Bear's Picnic. Each child was asked to bring a favorite teddy. Games were played while holding a teddy bear. "Goldilocks and the Three Bears" was acted out and read. A teddy bear cake was eaten.

A Pink Party. Everyone invited had to wear pink clothes from top to toes. Pink decorations lined the house. Pink food was eaten (pink Jello, pink ham sandwiches, pink milk, pink cake, and pink ice cream). Pink favors were given out.

You don't have to spend a lot of money to give kids a fun birthday party! Parties for young kids are easy. Choose simple indoor games in winter or water balloon games in the summer. As our first child got older, we planned a different type of party each year a tea party (the kids dressed up, and parents and siblings were waiters/waitresses), a surprise party, a mystery party (write your own "whodunit?"), or a video scavenger hunt (the kids, in groups, videotaped themselves doing the things on their list). Our second child has remembered which party was done in which grade for older siblings and has made those her choice as well. To help siblings of the birthday child feel special, include them in some of the plans, and give them a part in the party. Whatever you do, be enthusiastic. No matter how zany the activity, join in!

We have an alternate plan for birthday parties in our home, one that is especially nice for families who have several children and find it difficult to spend time one on one. I take whoever's birthday it is out of school for the day, and we go out for a fancy lunch, shopping, tea, or whatever just to spend the day together. My daughters quite often prefer this to a party.

- In our home we celebrate each child's birthday with immediate family by allowing the child to choose their favorite meal and cake, which Mom prepares. Birthday parties with friends are planned for every other year.

- My second son has a summer birthday, so he was never able to celebrate at school. One year I asked his teacher if we could celebrate his half-birthday. She agreed, so we had half a cupcake on half a plate, with half a napkin, half a cup of juice . . . you get the idea.

- Make life easier for yourself and give older siblings a chance to be creative by allowing an older sibling to plan, decorate, and run the games at the birthday party of a younger sibling. Usually the birthday king or queen and his/her friends love having the older children involved.

- After a certain age I stopped making birthday cakes in shapes of animals and other favorite characters and started making them in the shape of their new age. That way when I took pictures, I always had a record of which birthday it was.

- Since my daughter is sometimes invited to a party with little notice, and we do not have time to shop for a gift, I regularly keep a supply of birthday presents on hand. Several times a year my daughter assists me in shopping for these birthday gifts, which we store in a big box. Not only have we minimized stress, but we have also saved money, since many items in the gift box were purchased at terrific sale prices. All we have to do is wrap the gift. I also keep a supply of birthday cards on hand. (My mother taught me this by modeling it for me.) The gift box includes not only kids' birthday gifts but also Christmas gifts for nieces and nephews and special gifts for my friends such as note cards, bubble bath, or pretty napkins.

You can also fill a box with rice or noodles and let the kids search for small treasures you have hidden inside.

● On each child's birthday, I take their picture with their dad. Our children have small photo albums that are reserved for these photos. It's fun to look back and see how they've changed over the years (kids *and* dad!).

● On birthdays and half-birthdays our children were allowed to choose the menu, no holds barred, including the year my daughter invited her Pioneer Girls pal for dinner on her birthday and we served my daughter's menu choice— lasagna, mashed potatoes, and birthday cake! Generally, however, our children have come up with remarkably well balanced meals.

Scavenger hunts and bigger and better hunts are easy to put together, take a long time, and get the older kids out of the house for a while! Another good idea for boys is to buy a big stack of baseball cards, put them in the center of the floor with the boys sitting around them, and let the kids take turns drawing baseball cards from the pile. They love to examine each card and talk among themselves about the featured team and player.

● For a birthday party for kids ten and older a scavenger hunt is especially effective. They can collect natural objects out-side—a red stone, acorns, a pretty flower, or whatever—or go to neighbors' houses and ask for one object per house, small inexpensive things—a paper clip, a toothpick, a Pop-sicle stick, a penny with a certain date, a plastic utensil, a certain length of dental floss, a ketchup packet from a restaurant, a canceled stamp, or whatever.

While the kids are gone, parents can regroup, clean up the mess from games or gift openings, and set out the food. A variation on this idea is to have a sound scavenger hunt. You need two or three small tape recorders for this. Sounds that can be collected, one from each house, include: everyone in the house singing "Row, row, row your boat," an alarm clock, a dog barking, a music box, someone playing "Chopsticks" on the piano, a car horn, a man whistling "Dixie," a squeaky door, a child under six singing "Mary Had a Little Lamb," a toilet flushing.

● We announced the birthdays of our boys by tying a few balloons in a tree in the front yard. I told the boys it was our way of saying, "Guess what? Somebody here is celebrating!"

● I think birthdays should *always* be celebrated, and I have had parties of some kind every year for each of my children. As a result, each of them do creative and special things for my birthday and my husband's! I encouraged cards and gifts from every family member for each one's special day, and brothers and sisters were welcome to join in at their siblings' parties. When they were younger, I made whatever kind of cake they wanted: rainbows, G.I. Joe, Gummi Bears, three-layer Cinderella, race cars—and I am *not* a cake designer. I just had fun trying to make the cake that was ordered!

I also bought fun presents for all our little guests to take home. I set them out on the table and labeled each with a number. At the end of the party (after the kids had seen the numbered gifts on the table), I led them to our bathtub filled with water and floating boats with numbers underneath. Each child chose a boat, and their boat's number determined their take-home gift. What fun for the guests after seeing the birthday child get so many presents!

● We have a red-and-white dinner plate that is inscribed "Special Day Plate." The birthday person gets to use this on his/her special day, set on a red-and-white round place mat designed and quilted by my mother. This plate is also used to commemorate any special event in a family member's life. Several times we've used it to signal a meal during which we affirm what we like about the person being honored, an event called because that person needs cheering up.

For several years I made a birthday place mat following each child's birthday with a large piece of construction paper and their birthday cards. Then I covered the place mat with clear contact paper on each side and used the place mats for special occasions.

Creativity and fun are keys to this whole matter. Our children still talk with fond memories about the year that we planned treasure hunts for their birthday parties. They invited their friends, but *we* planned the party. Early in the day of the party, my husband and I went to the library and hid the first clue in some obscure book. The second we left with the management at Dairy Queen, and the next we delivered to the local popcorn shop. We gave the kids their initial instructions at home, which sent them off to the library. In the book they found their clue for Dairy Queen, where we had already paid for them to be served ice cream treats. The management handed them their next clue, which had them off and running to the popcorn shop. We ended the party at home with cake and ice cream. (The merchants got a big charge out of this plan as well!)

5

Books

~~~◯~~~

I remember the favorite books of all three of my boys—
books that were so well-worn that I have since purchased new
versions to save for years down the road when our children
have children. Chad's favorite was *The Little House*, Nathan's
was *Tikki Tikki Tembo*, and Jordan's was *Can't You Sleep, Little
Bear?* What is it about reading books that makes for such a
great time of mother and child bonding? Maybe it's the shared
adventures, the tender feelings, the laughs and giggles in all
the same places, and the little hands that curled around my
fingers while I was reading.

When I was pregnant with our first child, my mother-in-law
gave me a copy of the book *Honey for a Child's Heart*, which was
very enriching to read. The writer, Gladys Hunt, knows that

> truth and excellence have a way of springing up all over the
> world, and our role as parents is to teach our children how
> to find and enjoy the riches of God and to reject what is
> mediocre and unworthy of Him. . . . As Christian parents we
> are concerned about building whole people—people who are
> alive emotionally, spiritually, intellectually. The instruction to
> *train up a child in the way he should go* encompasses so much

more than teaching him the facts of the gospel. It is to train the child's character, to give him high ideals and to encourage integrity. It is to provide largeness of thought, creative thinking, imaginative wondering—an adequate view of God and His world. He can never really appreciate the finest without personal redemption. But many a redeemed person lives in a small insecure world because he has never walked with God into the larger place which is His domain. We have books and The Book at our disposal to use wisely for God's glory. A young child, a fresh uncluttered mind, a world before him—to what treasures will you lead him? With what will you furnish his spirit?[11]

Ideas from Other Moms

● When children are learning to read, make frequent trips to the library, let them pick out books, and choose some easy-reader books they can read to you. Sit and listen to them read daily. Be encouraging and patient, so it is an enjoyable time together.

● I place a high value on reading to my children. Even though Judd is an avid reader at age ten, he still enjoys having books read out loud to him. Reading together is such a great time to maintain the physical contact kids may otherwise be growing out of and to share some relaxed time together. It also gives them a chance to use their imagination in this age of video orientation. It also obviously serves them well in school.

● Garage sales were a good source of books for our family. Library books frequently got misplaced or sometimes drawn on, but the books we picked up at garage sales proved to be inexpensive, and I didn't care if they were spilled on or dog-eared. When the kids were younger, I scattered baskets of books around the house for easy access and easy clean-up.

Books have always been important in our family. When our first daughter was born, her daddy bought her *The Wind in the Willows*, even though she was only two days old! That started a tradition for all four daughters. Every birthday and Christmas, we buy each child a special book—always in hardcover so it will last. It might be a classic or part of a set. One child has the Beatrix Potter books, another The Little House on the Prairie series, and so on. By the time each child has their own children, they will have a wonderful collection to start their babies on. We have built up quite a library over the last sixteen years. We also have family reading times. Our sixteen-year-old still climbs on the bed with everybody else to hear Dad read a book. We've gone through the whole Narnia series, George MacDonald books, Max Lucado, etc. This is a wonderful way to teach biblical truths in a fun way.

I have read to my children from about age one month. There were many wonderful books that I started with. Most of them had pictures or were vocabulary books or had animals for which I made up the sounds. Every night, even at that early age, I read one story from Ken Taylor's *The Bible in Pictures for Little Eyes*, sang "Jesus Loves Me," and prayed with the children. As they outgrew that Bible story book, we went into Bible story books that had longer stories but continued to sing and pray. As soon as they could read, I bought an easy-reader Bible story book and had them read to me. Then we progressed to books like *Christian's Journey* by John Bunyan and The Chronicles of Narnia by C. S. Lewis for our bedtime reading.

When the children were quite small, my husband started reading the classics to them each night. They worked their way through a book at a time, reading a little each night.

Drawings of each character, sketched by Dad, were put in their rooms. Depending on the age level and attention span of the children, long descriptive passages were abbreviated and plots were frequently reviewed. Having three boys, we selected such novels as *Moby Dick*, *20,000 Leagues Under the Sea*, the Narnia series, and *Last of the Mohicans*, among others. Each child came away with the experiences that his or her age allowed; as each new novel was read, the experiences grew, and an appreciation for good literature was begun.

Our kids (when they were little) liked having us read books to them when driving on long trips. I can't read in the car because of motion sickness, so I put some of the kids' favorite books on tape. These books were not long; I didn't tackle books with chapters. I was able to add some music as well, hitting a pan with a spoon when it was time to turn the page. They got a kick out of hearing Mom on their tapes. Also, when my mother was diagnosed with terminal brain cancer, I was pregnant with my third child. We both knew the baby would not remember his grandmother (she died when my baby was ten weeks old). So I asked my mom to read some of our favorite books on tape for our new baby. She also talked to him at the beginning of the tape. I know this will be a priceless possession for my son.

When young children are learning to read, we should make lots of different books available. As they get older, I think it is important to be even more selective and steer them toward *great* literature—the classics, autobiographies, poetry, etc.

I have made my children's reading *my* concern. I loved to read as a child (still do), but I was exposed to some books that I had no business reading. So I have been careful to choose books for my daughters that contain acceptable subject matter and are good literature. One of our favorite authors (apart from obvious selections such as Thornton

Wilder, C. S. Lewis, George MacDonald, Frances Hodgson Burnett, J. R. R. Tolkien, etc.) is Marguerit De Angeli. *Thee, Hannah!, Henner's Lydia, Skippack School,* and more were written in the 1930s and 1940s. They're no longer in print but can be found in the library. They can be read to kindergartners and above and read by third graders.

Lois Lenski is another author we have enjoyed: *Strawberry Girl, Corn Farm Boy, Prairie School,* etc. My girls liked the regional books best, though she has written historical fiction as well. Cynthia Harnett has written some great historical fiction set in medieval England, appropriate for junior high: *The Great House, The Writing on the Hearth, The Merchant's Mark,* and others. Have you ever read the original, unedited *Pinocchio* by C. Collodi? It is a rich book, with many excellent lessons for the whole family. As you can see, children's literature is a real hot spot for me! I have enjoyed keeping a record of all the books my daughters have read, and it's been fun for them to go back and review it over the years.

I started a summer program of reading in order for my children to earn money for treats at the pool. The kids received pool money credit to the tune of a penny a minute. An hour of reading in the morning could easily mean a soda at the pool, but nachos with cheese took some serious reading time! You have never seen kids so happy to read—and a mom so happy to buy treats at the pool.

6

Calendars and Schedules

I once paged through my large calendar that I kept open on the kitchen desk, and came across one month that had fifty-eight entries of "extra" activities for our family of five. Those of you with your first newborn probably have less, and I'm sure many of you have more. Calendars and schedules are useful tools that assist us in our attempts to be organized, but they offer us no help in setting our priorities and our limits. We need to be thinking and praying about our priorities daily, *before* we come to our calendars.

> Hurried people are the ones who have said yes to so many things that now they seem to be on the verge of panic. Just observing their lives brings to mind the school-yard rhyme: When in trouble, when in doubt, run in circles, scream and shout.[12]

Psalm 39:4–7 encourages us to redirect our focus on the eternal.

> Lord, help me to realize how brief my time on earth will be. Help me to know that I am here for but a moment more. My life is no longer than my hand! My whole lifetime is but a moment

to you. Proud man! Frail as breath! A shadow! And all his busy rushing ends in nothing. He heaps up riches for someone else to spend. And so, Lord, my only hope is in you.

My Creator offers to give me wisdom about calendars, schedules, priorities, and limits. He had the challenge of a busy life when He was on earth too.

The kinds of complexities that tie most of us up in knots never seemed to concern Jesus. He kept His life focused by setting limits. He chose twelve (not twelve hundred) into whom He would pour His life for three years (He had an end date in mind). Rather than getting caught in the success trap that says bigger is better and that enough is never enough, He chose to own only those things He could easily carry with Him as He walked among the people. *His ability to set limits was the reason He could focus fully on the moment rather than fuss around with a million worrisome concerns.*[13]

May we learn from His example—spending time with the Father, focusing on eternal issues, and setting appropriate limits.

Ideas from Other Moms

● It's hard for me to remember things unless I can *see* them. I've always kept a small desk calendar, but one year my husband bought a big month-by-month laminated wall calendar and put it up on the inside of our kitchen cabinets. There was a small box for each day, and we wrote on it with dry-erase markers. At first I said there was no way we were keeping such an eyesore, but then I found it indispensable (after all, it was on the *inside* of the cabinets). It was easy to remember which weeks we would be out of town, important dates involving the whole family, etc. I think it will be even more helpful when my children get older and have important dates and a schedule of their own. By having one main family calendar, we make sure no one is double-booked or forgets what's coming up. Different colored markers are used for each family member.

● Concerning my own personal calendar, for fourteen years I have purchased the same calendar at the local stationery store. It's a weekly calendar appearing on two pages, and it's also hourly up until 6 P.M., with a space for each evening. I not only write down my schedule, but also what I know of the children's appointments and meetings. What I don't know about, the older kids and my husband fill in. (They are required to do that if they want me to help them remember or if I have to take them somewhere.) I could never function without this system. Everyone in the family refers to it. I'm so dependent on it that I blow a gasket if someone runs off with it! If it's not on the calendar, it's not happening! We encourage our oldest and busiest to let us know about extra quiz practices, birthday parties, baby-sitting obligations, etc. *ahead* of time.

● It is certainly advisable to check the calendar before committing to new responsibilities. Furthermore, don't say yes just because the time is free. Look at the days surrounding the date in question so you know if the event you're considering will add more stress than you want. Nobody else knows what our comfort zones are regarding stress, so we must learn our limits and stick to them! We owe this not only to ourselves, but to our husbands and children.

● When I was working outside the home, my calendar was my brain; it helped me keep my life together. I thought having a lot of "free" time when I was at home as a mother would be a welcome change from the frantic schedule I was living. But after I had my first child, I found that I never had much free time and that days could slip by without seeing anyone other than my husband and son. Being a mother can lead to isolation. The empty calendar I had anticipated was not always a good thing. I didn't realize how difficult it would be to make plans with other people. Leaving things to chance doesn't seem to work, because there will always be something to eat up my time at home.

I have learned that I need to schedule a few things and to get them on the calendar in advance. If I don't do this, weeks can go by without seeing my friends. It has been important to be involved in a few regularly scheduled activities like a women's Bible study, a couples' Bible study, and a local MOPS (Mothers of Pre-schoolers) group. Remaining in fellowship with others has been essential to my spiritual and personal growth.

● My husband travels a great deal, and my small children have a hard time grasping how long Daddy will be gone. So before leaving on a trip, my husband makes up a small calendar for them, with a box for each day that he is gone. Their planned activities are listed in the boxes. On extended trips he also leaves them a small present to open each day while he is away. These measures make his absence much more manageable for the children.

● It's amazing how many times each day I refer to my calendar to make sure I'm not forgetting something I'm supposed to be doing! Something that has helped me visually is to color code my children's activities when I write them on my calendar. I bought ballpoint pens with different colored inks (pink, aqua, green), and each child gets his own color when I write in appointments, games and practices, lessons, etc. The month looks very colorful as I check my calendar daily!

● A few years ago our extended family came up with the idea of a family calendar as well. They are so easy to do now with the right computer program. Each family is assigned a month. This includes my grandfather, my parents, two sets of aunts and uncles, seven cousins, and ourselves. We each make a collage of our year in photos on an 8 x 11 sheet of paper and send it to the coordinator. They bind it with the calendar, which includes everyone's birthdays and anniversaries. It's fun to look at various relatives' pictures (ranging from Washington State to Boston) for a month each year. We feel so much more in touch with their everyday lives this way.

● Schedules are just as crucial for children as for their parents. They need to know that certain things are done at certain times. I believe this contributes to their feelings of security, happiness, and rest. Having a schedule doesn't mean we have to be inflexible, but it is a good guide for a less stressful life.

● Our three children have always been early risers. In their preschool and early elementary school years it was not uncommon for them to be up and ready to play by 4:30 A.M., no matter what time they had gotten to bed the night before. In the interest of self-preservation, we made a house rule that if they had tried to go back to sleep after awakening early and couldn't, they could read or play quietly in their own rooms until 6:30. They were not to leave their rooms before then except to visit the bathroom. One morning several weeks after we had begun to enforce this new rule, I awoke to hear playful voices outside our bedroom. Annoyed, I slipped out of bed and opened the door, ready to scold them for ignoring the new rule and waking me up at such an early hour. They were playing with toy cars in the hallway, but each one smiled at me as I emerged from the bedroom. I had to laugh when I saw what they were up to. You see, they knew they were in complete compliance with the rule to stay in their rooms because each child had been sure to keep one foot over the threshold of his doorway!

7

Car Trips

⁓꧑⁓

For many years Jim and I and our boys drove down to Florida over spring break. My parents owned a condominium on the beach and graciously let us use it each year. So we drove twenty-six hours southeast and twenty-six hours northwest each trip—well worth the memories of smelling the sweet orange groves on the Florida Turnpike, going back and forth from the ocean to the pool, hunting for shells, swimming to the sandbar, seeing the squid wash up on the beach, and going to Krispie Kreme for doughnuts.

We actually looked forward to our time in the car—unwinding and being together. We were not the picture-perfect family who sang and played games all the way there and back. Our approach was to think of things each family member likes and to encourage them to bring those along for the car ride. Our motto was: "Take along three times as much as you think you might need!" A few days before leaving on the trip, we made visits to the library and bookstore, making sure each family member had plenty of reading material. Everyone's favorite drinks and snacks were loaded into the cooler. When the kids were younger, they brought stuffed animals, art projects, and snap-tight models. As you can imagine, the inside of our ve-hicle never qualified for a neatness award on these trips, but the emphasis was on keeping everyone content doing what they like to do.

Ideas from Other Moms

● When our children were little and all three in car seats, we put the twins in the third seat of our mini-van with a laundry basket full of toys and books in between them. We did the same for our third child in the other seat. They were happy as could be. By the time they had emptied the basket and were getting restless, it was time for a rest stop anyway. We picked the toys up from the floor, reloaded the baskets, and were ready to go again. We also played a lot of sing-along tapes and enjoyed family singing. Now that our children are older, we enjoy borrowing library tapes and listening to mysteries on trips. We also enjoy playing geography, word, and mental math games.

● After years of car trips, telling the kids we're leaving at such and such a time (only to roll out of the driveway an hour later), I now have a different approach. When the kids say, "What time are we leaving?" I respond, "We'll leave when we're ready." They seem to be more patient and helpful in getting the show on the road.

● When taking trips in the car, buy several new play items to pull out one at a time. Pack reclosable containers of nibble food items to distribute. Have preschoolers put Cheerios on a string to make a necklace, then wear them and eat them!

● Each day of traveling vacations, encourage the children to pick out and buy a postcard of a place they enjoyed. Have them write on the back of the postcard what they did that day and any additional thoughts or feelings. This promotes writing skills, but it also becomes a memory of the trip that they will enjoy in the years to come. For kids too young to write, have them tell you what they enjoyed about that day and write it on the postcard for them.

● When traveling with multiple children, rotate the seating arrangement every hour or so.

● Use seat belts! Our family travels frequently on long trips around the country, and we have very young children. We find there is little commotion when they are safely tucked into one small area of the car. Each child brings a back-pack of things to do: crayons, paper, books, tape players, games, etc.

● Now that our children are getting older, we get tapes from the library of old radio shows, which our kids think are hi-larious, as well as books on tape. We have also read books together in the car—for example, *Where the Red Fern Grows*. Each person who is old enough to read takes a turn reading out loud. Our family looks forward to long trips.

● Our children really enjoyed the pocket trays I purchased for them on our last car trip. Pencils, markers, paper, etc. can be stored in the two side pockets. Mom can use it, too! I did all my Christmas cards one year during a thirteen-hour car trip over Thanksgiving.

● On *long* car trips, we made a box with suction cups to stick on the window next to the kids. Inside we put toys like koosh balls, little books, pipe cleaners, paper, and colored pencils.

● Is there a car big enough for six people? When our children were young, we took a lot of driving trips. We usually toured for a week, then stayed at a beach cottage for a week. The kids always loved to listen to their tapes—not once, but a hundred times. One trip, my husband and I became tired of listening to Tom Sawyer bumbling around in a dark, drippy cave, so we came up with an idea. Larry went to Radio Shack and purchased four inexpensive headsets with extremely long cords and one adapter to plug them into. The kids listened to their beloved stories for the 101st time, and Larry and I had sweet peace!

When we leave on a trip, the first thing we do in the driveway before backing out is to pray, asking God not only for safety as we travel, but that our house would stay safe while we're gone. This has become kind of a tradition. It's been fun to hear the girls say, "I'll pray, I'll pray" as we're closing doors and getting seat belts on!

Give young children a box or can of assorted Band-Aids and let them customize the back windows of the car. It takes a long time to open them all, and the Band-Aids can be moved around creatively for a long time!

Whenever we took a trip with young children, I bought at least one new toy or game especially for that trip. For many years it was a box of *Colorforms*, because they keep a child occupied for many hours, are lightweight, pack easily, and are fairly inexpensive.

8

Challenges, Needs, and Stages of Motherhood

An Interview with Three Christian Counselors

Doreen's mom had been extremely overprotective and compulsive, and her father had been consumed with his career. She experienced many fears in her childhood years, although she was too young to understand what was going on at the time. As with any youngster, she assumed that all families were like this. She went off to college, married, and started her own family. In her early years of motherhood, her dad left her mom for another woman, quickly divorcing and remarrying. This precipitating event brought pain and instability into Doreen's life, raising all kinds of questions about her family of origin, her own marriage and family, and how she was now going to manage relationships with her grieving mom, her dad and new wife, and her own siblings.

This is a true-to-life example of a young mom who grew up in a family with unfinished business. The older I get, the more I discover that each of us has our own stories and our own needs. Some needs are common to moms at particular stages of family life. Other situations have more to do with unaddressed and unresolved issues from the past that keep popping up to say hello. Whatever the situation, we can't afford to ignore destructive feelings or behaviors that continue to plague us, because they don't usually go away on their own and often lead to bigger problems later on. The following interview speaks to such situations.

What brings moms to you? What are some of the common needs in a mom's life? What are some of the typical stages moms can expect to pass through? I asked these questions of Ruth Gibson, Mary Ryken, and Joan Stough, three Christian women who are professional counselors. Their information could easily become a book of its own, but for our purposes here I will summarize their comments and insights as concisely and helpfully as possible.

The common denominator of all the reasons for seeking counsel is problems in relationships. Mary observed that women are typically the "custodians" of relationships.

> Women are the barometers of family tensions and anxieties, and it should surprise no one that it is women, rather than men, who most often seek therapy for themselves, their marriages, and their children.[14]

Joan reports that it's almost always the woman in a marriage who calls first. When the husband/father is the first one to call, it's often after things have escalated so much that the relationships are at the point of no return. Even though Joan prefers to see both husband and wife for marital issues, she realizes that one is better than none. Unfortunately, the circumstances prompting women to call Ruth are often the extramarital affairs of their husbands and the resulting pain the women are experiencing. She likes and recommends Jerry Jenkins's book *Loving Your Marriage Enough to Protect It* and thinks that behavioral safeguards should be discussed and practiced by husbands and wives.

Joan sees depression most often at two different stages of the mother's life cycle—when a young mom has toddlers at home and during the empty nest years. She observes more such depression among non-working moms. According to Frank Minirth and Paul Meier in their book *Happiness Is a Choice*, the symptoms of depression fall into five main categories:

1. Moodiness, sadness, crying or feeling like crying frequently.
2. Painful thinking: overly introspective in a self-derogatory way.
3. Physical symptoms: sleep changes, appetite changes, headaches, and others.
4. Anxiety or agitation; irritability, trouble sitting still.
5. Delusional thinking, out of touch with reality (this is an advanced stage).[15]

Difficulties with children account for a large number of counseling situations. Ruth feels that often what a child needs is more of the parent—more of their laps when the child is small, and more of their eyes and ears when they are older. We need wisdom to know when to be closely involved and when to turn responsibility over to the child. Mary perceives that women often make themselves responsible for the people around them in order to feel productive or useful or to have a sense of identity. If these women see their role as creating happiness around them and things are going well, they're fine. But when things go wrong, they become unhappy. She also believes that counseling helps women see where their appropriate control begins and ends—what they are responsible for and what they're not. Unhealthy forms of "responsibility" include maneuvering, manipulating, or being a go-between.

Other troubling situations that all three women see are the pain of infertility, loneliness, anxiety from a fast-paced lifestyle, and job stress. Many moms express their feelings of inadequacy to Joan. She smiled when she commented that for the Christian woman, this feeling can be a blessing because our sense of inadequacy can be a catalyst that sends us back to our source of wisdom and strength—the God of heaven.

What are the biggest needs of moms, as you see them? was my second question for Ruth, Mary, and Joan. Once again I discovered some common denominators in their responses. These include the need for *meaning and significance* in life, the need for *identity*, the need for *healthy relationships*, and the need to take *personal responsibility*.

All three counselors believe that finding meaning and significance in life is first found in our relationship with God. In spite of the fact that we are flawed people, He loves us and wants a relationship with us. If we can feel secure in that relationship, we have a sense of worth and contentment, along with a proper perspective and purpose for life.

And may you be able to feel and understand, as all God's children should, how long, how wide, how deep, and how high his love really is; and to experience this love for yourselves, though it is so great that you will never see the end of it or fully know or understand it. And so at last you will be filled up with God himself. Now glory be to God who by his mighty power at work within us is able to do far more than we would ever dare to ask or even dream of—infinitely beyond our highest prayers, desires, thoughts or hopes.

EPHESIANS 3:18–20

The need for personal identity is a strong one, according to Ruth, Mary, and Joan. Each of them encourages moms to develop their own personal gifts and abilities. Every mom needs her own interests and roles beyond the family as well as inside it. Each counselor cautioned against the mom who so totally involves herself in her family that she loses her own personhood and becomes depressed. Carefully chosen outside interests and responsibilities, on the other hand, can enhance a mom's contribution to her family and her future. I remember being asked to serve on the Music & Worship Committee at church back when our children were very young. I'm not sure who benefited more—the church or me. The benefit to the church was that I worked hard and enjoyed my contribution of service. I was also the beneficiary in that I was affirmed by being asked, and it was a good chance to broaden my horizons as a young mom.

The need for healthy relationships, as I mentioned earlier, is the need that often brings us in to see a counselor. Friendships built through common interests and shared experiences are necessary at all stages of motherhood. I value my friends who have seen me at my best and at my worst and like me just the same. Mary observed that from a very early age girls typically like having a "best friend." This exhibits their desire for closeness and intimacy, a need that stays with women for their whole lives. One morning I went for a walk and came up behind two ladies who were probably in their seventies. They were obviously having a wonderful time—talking, laughing, and gesturing with their hands. We need friends for the good times and the hard times.

Joan hears women speak of their need to love, nurture, and be needed by those around them. Ruth believes women need the affirmation, time, and faithfulness of their husbands. Learning to communicate directly and asking people around us for what we need is a topic on which counselors typically spend large amounts of time.

> Most women who enter therapy, regardless of the nature of the presenting problem, need help primarily in balancing their own needs with those of other family members.[16]

Another category of need that surfaced in my interviews with Ruth, Mary, and Joan was that of moms taking personal responsibility for their own happiness throughout their lives and relationships, rather than depending on someone else to make them happy. It is self-defeating when moms see themselves as victims. We would do well to be concerned with our purposeful *acting* as opposed to merely *reacting* to those around us. We need to take personal responsibility for slowing our lives down and clearing out what's not necessary. Too often we don't leave ourselves enough "processing time," as Ruth calls it. We need some elbow room, and we shouldn't wait for others to provide it for us.

Extra needs that they added included supportive extended families, encouragement from older women, and a willingness to see life as cycles and stages.

> Many joinings and separations occur in the course of the family life cycle—from singleton independence to couple interdependence, incorporation of triadic dependence, partial separations, and exits with achievement of full independence.[17]

What stages can moms typically expect to pass through? was the third question I posed to Ruth, Mary, and Joan. The months of pregnancy or the process of adoption define the first stage of motherhood. Joan calls this the "anticipation and preparation" stage.

> Given the importance of parenting, it is remarkable that most mothers and fathers receive so little preparation for this role. Most learn to parent "on the job," an inefficient and often discouraging process.[18]

The months of anticipation can be a useful and helpful time for the mother-to-be. Reading books with her husband on child-rearing and discussing them provide a tremendous start. I had a difficult time sleeping at night in the last couple of months of each pregnancy. Just rolling over was a major endeavor—I felt that a crane would have been helpful! When I couldn't sleep, I decided it was part of God's preparation for the middle-of-the-night feedings yet to come, so I got up and sat in the nursery rocking chair. Some nights I read parenting books, some nights I sang through a songbook of lullabies given to me as a shower gift, and other nights I read the Bible, God's best instruction manual for parents.

> You made all the delicate, inner parts of my body, and knit them together in my mother's womb. Thank you for making me so wonderfully complex! It is amazing to think about. Your workmanship is marvelous—and how well I know it. You were there while I was being formed in utter seclusion! You saw me before I was born and scheduled each day of my life before I began to breathe. Every day was recorded in your Book!
>
> PSALM 139:13–16

Names given to the next stage were "baby and toddler years," "early years," or "preoccupation years"—in short, the years when the kids are babies and toddlers, hanging close to Mom. This is a crucial stage for setting patterns of good behavior, building healthy parent-child relationships, and encouraging children to have confidence and competence. It's also a fun stage, though one that is enormously challenging.

> Pregnancy offers nine months to get ready for motherhood, but there is little in a woman's previous life experience to prepare her for the reality of being totally responsible for the welfare of an infant. Although motherhood is deeply satisfying for most women, a child's need for round-the-clock nurturance stretches beyond the capacity of any one person. The frequency of postpartum depression, particularly after the birth of the first child, is often thought to be triggered by a hormonal imbalance. However, it may also reflect the woman's sense of loss of her former freedom and the overwhelming nature of her new responsibilities. Her sense of losing her connectedness to the outside world may be especially strong if she has left her job to devote her energies to full-time motherhood. In addition, the birth of a child requires that a woman rework many of the important relationships in her life.[19]

Ruth, Mary, and Joan all encourage women at this stage to make some time for themselves and to be purposeful in pursuing an outside activity or project that is of interest to them.

Ruth labeled the period when the kids are in school the "bleacher years," the years that moms are taking children hither and yon to school, sports, music lessons, and other activities that keep us watching them from the bleachers. The latter half of these years is commonly known to us all as "adolescence." Joan describes this as the stage that "keeps moms humble and honest."

> Adolescence is something that happens to a family, not just to an individual child. The family boundaries, having remained fairly stable around the nuclear and extended family for twelve or thirteen years, are suddenly required to develop the elasticity necessary to alternately let adolescents go, shelter their retreats, and encompass the barrage of people and ideas they bring into the family from the outside. Their pushing and pulling in family relationships goes through the system with a domino effect.[20]

Joan emphasizes that it is important for the adolescent to *differentiate* himself or herself from his parents in order to consolidate his or her own identity and prepare for a healthy adulthood. Moms who understand this as a necessary developmental task will be less likely to experience this as personal rejection.

All three counselors saw the next stage as the off-to-college or career years. Joan calls it "renegotiation." The kids have been pushing away from the parent, but now they begin the process of reconnecting as peers. "I feel like I am being involuntarily retired from a job that I like!" was the way Mary heard one woman describe this stage. Mary has observed that the struggle of letting go is more difficult if our relationships are struggling. Ruth speaks of letting go in a book she wrote with her husband, *The Sandwich Years*.

> Most of us in the sandwich years are past the days of cuddling our babies, bandaging grade schoolers' skinned knees, and dealing with our inscrutable teenagers. Now we face an even tougher job—affirming their independence as adults. Letting go—detaching—is what it's all about. We will always be their

parents, but how we play that role will change, just as *they* have changed in what they need from us.[21]

Post-college and career years might be described as a period of "readjustment." We don't stop being moms when our kids marry and begin their own families; so this segment of life can be a struggle in terms of learning the proper level of involvement in our children's lives. It's easy to become intrusive and attempt to get too involved. Our children don't necessarily take the paths we've always wanted them to take. We might expect them to live nearby, be home for every holiday, and be "successful" as we define it. They might move away, be home for few holidays, and go a different direction than what we had ever imagined.

Relating as adults and friends goes pretty smoothly if we feel comfortable with their choices. Things have the potential to get bumpy, however, if we don't like their choices. That's where readjusting comes in. We may need to set aside some of the expectations or dreams we had for them. Extending some of our mothering impulses *outside* our family at this time can be healthy. For example, if her children have moved away, a middle-aged mom might come alongside a younger woman to offer encouragement and give help when the younger mom is overburdened. As with any of the stages of motherhood, readjustment will not likely be the same for any two children— giving us lots of room for growth in flexibility!

My time with Ruth, Mary, and Joan has given me new understanding and encouragement about the challenges, needs, and stages of motherhood. Besides the important resources of our relationship with God, husbands, families, and close friendships, we can benefit from the insights and understanding of a Christian counselor at various stages of our motherhood experience. I encourage moms to consider counseling if they come to speedbumps in life they just can't seem to get over even after repeated attempts to back up and give their cars a little more gas!

9

Clothing

~~~

Children's clothing is an interesting commentary on the stages of childhood. I've saved a few favorites in one of my dresser drawers—a small pair of saddle shoes, a hat, and a Superman undershirt. I remember a red plaid sports jacket that Chad wore when he was four. (He was wearing it the evening of his violin recital when he dropped his violin *twice*; we have the incident on video, and every now and then we threaten to send it off to a video contest!) I remember the four baby showers given for my first child by family, Sunday school class, neighbors, and fellow choir members. With all those showers, it seemed like this child wouldn't need anything for a *long* time. I'm guessing that his shower and baby gifts outfitted him for the first two years of his life, and Nate was able to use them as well, along with new gifts. Having stretched financially to buy a home, we didn't have much money to spend on clothes when the kids were little, so I sewed a lot of overalls and even made a Sunday suit or two.

During college, high school, and late grade school, all I saw going through the laundry were jeans, T-shirts, and sweats! Isn't it amazing how each child has his own tastes? After years of buying for them and shopping with them, I have a *pretty* good idea of what each one likes and dislikes.

My philosophy on buying clothes is simple—only seven words. Buy the minimum and wash a lot!

Ideas from Other Moms

Children

● Young children enjoy dressing themselves, so we installed a closet organizer and small-child-size hangers. Our children can now reach their own clothes. The clothes we don't want them to wear on a daily basis are placed on the high rack, so that our assistance is needed to get to them. I find it easier to keep track of clothes by hanging them all up rather than stuffing them in drawers. We hang all their pants up, too. Most stores let us keep the plastic hangers children's clothing come on.

● For my younger children, I purchased two small carts with open storage shelves for their clothing. As preschoolers just learning to dress themselves, this allowed easy access to their clothes. The key for young children is helping them to achieve the task of getting dressed independently.

● Children need parental guidance in coordinating their clothing on Sundays and special occasions. Taking an active interest in how our child looks is a way of demonstrating that we care about them. For everyday clothing, children should be allowed the *freedom* to select their own clothes within the confines of what's acceptable or not acceptable. This helps to foster independence and self-esteem. Children *do* view clothing as an extension of themselves, especially as they get older.

● We don't permit arguing over clothing and what to wear. The young child gets their choice of what to wear three days a week, and Mom or Dad selects clothing the other days. As the child gains experience and gets older, he or she can make decisions on more days. This eliminates arguments, especially on Sunday.

- When our girls were young, my husband and I figured we would choose their clothes through junior high. We reasoned that kids who chose their own clothes would have regrets when, as adults, they viewed pictures of their junior-high days. My kids don't think this is a good idea. They say that half the fun of looking back at their pictures will be seeing how *weird* they looked!

- Rather than just taking the kids out for back-to-school clothes shopping, we first sit down and explain to each child how many dollars are available for their wardrobe. They can spend it all on one outfit or they can shop for bargains and buy several—the decision is theirs. It is amazing how frugal a teenager can become if they are spending their "own" money! They make the decisions as to what is too expensive, rather than the parents having to be the "bad guys."

- I have two criteria for my children's clothing requests: reasonable cost and modesty. When my kids want clothing that we can't afford, they either spend their own money or we shop garage sales. There have been many styles that have come and gone for my kids from tots to teens, but as long as they use appropriate modesty, I let them choose clothes that help them feel comfortable and attractive.

- My husband and I feel it is extremely important to teach good money management to our children while they are in our home. The U.S. government certainly isn't a good example, and high schools rarely offer courses on this subject. Money mismanagement can cause lots of stress and even break up a marriage. Or, if done well, money management can help to further Christ and His kingdom! Upon completion of fourth grade, each of our children started making clothing purchases as they saw fit, using their clothing allowance. The amount of money given them per month for clothing varied with age, gender, and our family situation. We started with a "guesstimate" and changed the amount as necessary. The beauty of this plan has been hassle-free shopping with my children. If they want to buy some clothes and they have enough money in their "account," that's fine with me! They've learned that money goes a lot farther if you take advantage of sales and discount-type stores. They are also learning that when the money is gone in the middle of the month, they have to *stop* buying. It's like eating to the bottom of the cookie jar. When the supply is gone, it's gone! As they learn self-discipline, self-denial, delayed gratification, and patience, they are learning important lessons for life.

Mothers

Since I don't want my son to be embarrassed to introduce me to his friends, I try to keep up with the latest styles! I was always proud of my mom because she consistently looked nice, and I want to do the same for my family.

I heard Elisabeth Elliot Leitsch say something unexpected recently. Usually she's writing or talking about significant spiritual matters, but I was also delighted to hear her give some advice about a practical matter—clothes. She said that whenever she buys a new outfit, she also removes an old one from her closet. Why keep an outfit in your closet after a whole year of not wearing it? Also, in *Disciplines of a Beautiful Woman* Anne Ortlund urges us to "eliminate and concentrate." I try to eliminate old clothes from my closet about once a year.

My goal in purchasing clothing for myself is to dress in a way that feels attractive to me, is modest, and stays within our means financially. I have found beautiful items at garage sales, as well as store sales. I believe this is a personal matter for each woman and that no one should judge another as vain for wanting to look nice. My husband and my children appreciate my choices in clothing and my attention to personal appearance.

10

College

"$\mathcal{S}$ending a youngster to college these days is very educational. It teaches parents how to do without a lot of things."[22] Having just mailed another of our college payments toward our youngest son's education, I agree! When I first compiled the material for *The Christian Mom's Idea Book*, I particularly appreciated the ideas and suggestions from friends who had "been there" and "done that," since I was dealing with it for the first time. Perhaps the most helpful thing I did then was to read the book *Give Them Wings* by Carol Kuykendall. I read it at the end of Chad's junior year of high school, and earlier would have been even better!

Ideas from Other Moms

● I wish I were an expert on sending children off to college. I sent my first to school last year, and my last one leaves this year. The greatest joy of my life has been being a mom, and

I expected this time of my life to be devastating; but having kids away at college has not been as bad as I expected. Sure, I miss the day-to-day conversation and knowing what their life is like in detail. And yet some of that is good, too. If we look back to our growing-up years, we did some dumb things we were just as glad our parents didn't know about, and we survived.

As I analyze my parenting skills—a reflection that comes naturally when I feel like those years are coming to an end—I find that one thing I think my husband and I did right was to allow our children to make decisions for themselves as they grew up. The process was slow and different with each child, depending on their maturity level and the amount of trust each had achieved. Sometimes we let them make poor choices on things that were not harmful (like handling their own money, doing their own laundry, scheduling their own time, setting an alarm and getting themselves up, and being responsible for homework and papers without Mom's nagging).

It's hard to give our children the freedom to make mistakes, especially when we suspect they might choose poorly in a situation. However, we all learn by mistakes, and what better place to make the first ones than in the safety of home with "wise" parents who can talk kids through the consequences without saying, "I told you so." If we have watched our children learn lesson after lesson from both good and bad decisions, it is easier to let them go, because we have confidence in their decision-making skills. That is not to say that we won't still worry and have to daily put them in God's hands, but being prepared to let them go does make the separation less painful.

An enlarged phone budget is helpful for the off-to-college years. By talking to our students a few times a week, they feel connected with home, and we feel a little less separated.

Remember that by their senior year in high school, they are not home all that much anyway—between school, friends, sports, work, and youth group. And there are benefits to an empty nest—less people to cook for, fewer schedules to plan around, and when we clean the house, it stays that way! "To every thing there is a season, and a time for every purpose under the heaven" (Eccles. 3:1, KJV).

In planning ahead for the time when our children will leave home, probably for college, and be on their own, we've tried to give them more and more independence throughout high school, so that by the time they're seniors, they're making their own decisions. This is while we're still around for advice, help, or more teaching, if needed. For example, we want our children to have their own charge card in high school. Why? So they will learn how to use one *properly*. They need to learn about savings accounts and checking accounts. We let them suggest what time they'll come in at night. If it sounds too late, we'll talk about it. So far they've used good judgment.

As I read the local paper, I cut out articles that I think my college student would get a kick out of reading and send them off to her. It helps her feel connected, and she says it's provided her with some interesting dinnertime conversations with other students that come from our community.

I miss my son who's away at college, but I also miss seeing his friends that he hung around with in high school, who are also off to college. So every now and then I bake a big batch of cookies, freeze them (they pack better), and send some to my son and some to his friends.

I was not looking forward to the thought of taking our firstborn to college and saying good-bye, although she had been so busy and gone from the house so much her senior year of high school that I felt we had been "practicing" for a year. One thing that helped the good-bye tremendously was taking advantage of parent orientation the weekend we took her to college. We went to a brunch, a picnic, and several activities and had a chance to meet lots of teachers. By the time we left, we had real peace about leaving her there, and the good-bye wasn't as hard as we had expected. We felt that she was really ready!

The first time our daughter came home from college, we immediately saw our roles changing. Do you remember what it was like in high school chemistry when you added one chemical to another and got a chemical reaction? Well, that's what things were like at our house the first time she came home. Add something different to the mix, and the whole family dynamic changes. She figured that whatever she was used to doing at college (party mode, nocturnal hours) was fine to do at home. We weren't quite prepared for it; it caught us by surprise. So before she came home for the summer, my husband and I talked about setting reasonable expectations, and we discussed them with her on the ride home from college. Some of the topics included money, hours, and sibling relations. Setting expectations ahead of time was extremely helpful.

I think sending our first son off to college is the hardest thing I have done in my life so far. Talk about a point of no return. I knew he was ready for it, and I was happy with where he was going to school, but I couldn't believe how his going away broke my heart. I realized our family would never be the same. I will never stop missing him, but I am getting adjusted to his not being here. We have been pleased to have him home a few times, and despite warnings from other people of how much kids change once they leave home, we have found him to be the same as always—maturing nicely, but the same son we knew and loved. The best advice I can give to other moms is to try and have the heart-to-heart talk you have always been meaning to have before you send your son or daughter off. The night before we left on that equally dreaded and anticipated trip to school, my son and I had the talk that wrapped up the previous chapter of our lives and laid the groundwork for the chapter to come.

Now that my daughter has gone to college, do you know what her empty room reminds me of? That she needs all the prayer I can give! So as I continue on into my son's room to put some clean, folded clothes in his dresser, I bring my daughter before the Lord in prayer, thinking of her classes, friends, and other needs.

11

Communication

$\mathcal{W}$e don't have to go far to find examples of unhealthy communication patterns. There's the aggressive person who likes to pick a fight . . . the passive person who clams up and sometimes gives the silent treatment . . . the passive/aggressive person who uses sarcasm against others . . . the manipulative person who attempts to control others with fear. We could probably pin these different approaches on people in our circle of acquaintances without too much trouble. Sadly but honestly, some of these are *us*!

> We will lovingly follow the truth at all times—
> speaking truly, dealing truly, living truly—and so
> become more and more in every way like Christ
> who is the Head of his body, the church.
> EPHESIANS 4:15–16

If we're honest, communication with family and friends poses challenges for all of us from time to time. One of the most helpful tools Jim and I have tried to pass on to our boys is the AAA approach to communication in any challenging situation.

This plan comes straight out of Henry Virkler's book, *Speaking Your Mind Without Stepping on Toes*.[23]

The first A stands for *Affirmation*. In spite of the fact that we may disagree with a person or have difficulty with some aspect of his or her behavior, it's important to let him or her know that we respect him or her as a person. If we truly believe God created us in His image, then our communication must be mutually respectful, speaking the truth in love. But it's so hard to live this way consistently! I ask God for help in this area a lot.

The second A stands for *Assertion*.

- Describe the specific behavior that is causing frustration.
- Identify how I feel about the behavior.
- Speak in terms of specific behaviors, *not* personality characteristics.
- Avoid using the words *never* or *always*.

The third A stands for *Action*. I need to indicate to the other person how I would like to see his or her behavior change. It is appropriate to make a request. It is not appropriate to make demands. The request for action should correlate with the assertion that was made. Here's an example from our family. It hasn't been unusual for me, when I want to get the attention of one of the boys, to call to them (to shout) from the bottom of the stairs, top of the stairs, or end of the hallway. I don't like it when *they* do it, so I shouldn't be doing it, but I do sometimes. So one time Nate said, "Mom, I appreciate all you do for us, but it really bothers me when you yell up the stairs for me to come to dinner. Would you please come and get me instead?" There's the AAA approach in healthy action. He wasn't sarcastic about it—he didn't yell at me—he didn't give me the silent treatment. He affirmed me, asserted what was bothering him, and asked for a reasonable change. And I'm trying to make progress in this area! Speaking the truth in love (Ephesians 4:16) is not always easy, but it's healthy, it's right, and it's God's plan for showing mutual respect to one another.

Ideas from Other Moms

- A bit of advice I was given at a parenting seminar was this: Don't say anything to your child that you wouldn't say to a friend, because children deserve respect.

- A listening technique of which I'm a fan is *reflective listening*. It's explained in many communication-oriented publications. I can't say that I always practice it well (just ask my family), but when I employ it, there is usually much more open communication between the children and me. An example I can think of is if a child were to spout, "I don't ever want to play with Sam again! He and I were playing basketball together, and then when Danny came, the two of them went off together, even though I suggested all three of us could play!" A natural response on the part of the parent might run along the lines of, "Well, just find someone else to play with! There are plenty of other kids outside." But a parent employing reflective listening might respond, "Sounds like you're feeling pretty lonely and angry right now." This kind of statement encourages dialogue that may lead to some problem-solving, in contrast to the earlier statement, which basically is just the parent giving advice.

- When my children were preschoolers and I heard things other children had done that I wanted my children to avoid, I told them stories. By using fictitious names and starting with "Once upon a time," I told the story with its consequences. Examples: a child standing in the bathtub slipped and knocked out his tooth; or a little girl cut her own hair and had to get a "pixie" haircut. This was a *fun* way to warn my children of various situations. I told stories in the car, at bath time, and whenever we needed to do a mundane chore. Warning: They asked for these stories over and over and over!

● Schedule a monthly date with each child—a private one-on-one time. What to do and where to go are the child's choice. Always include some sitting and eating time to share. The talk of a preschooler is many times silly, but we are building a relationship in which the child will want to continue communicating as he or she grows older.

● I've had so many people tell me they wished they had written down the funny things their kids said that I took them seriously. Ever since the children first formed words, I have been journaling the funny things they've said, and I've since entered all the stories on our computer. Not only is this worth the effort just for posterity's sake, but it is so much fun for *them*; nothing delights them more than to laugh at the funny things they said when they were "younger."

● Children watch our response to death to see how they should act. If we know someone close is dying, it's good to talk to our children about the facts, but also about how we are working through it. It's helpful to share our feelings and to ask for theirs. Depending on their age, we need to be careful about how much we share; but they need to see how we hurt and how our faith fits in.

Don't be afraid to talk about heaven—kids want to know what the next step is, and this information will reassure them! A booklet called *Heaven* by Jo Bayly can open up some great family discussion. It's okay to cry in front of kids; that gives them permission to cry themselves.

After someone dies, make deliberate efforts to talk about the person who died. Memories help us heal, and kids want to remember the good times with their loved ones, though they will be hesitant to talk about him or her without our example. Bring the loved one into conversation in as easy and comfortable a manner as possible. If we cry over a good memory, sharing it is healthy. Helping our children work through death helps *us* heal too!

● Treating our children with respect is one of the most important things we parents can do. Remembering that toddlers and preschoolers have feelings and ideas that deserve respect can do much for their self-esteem. By showing respect to our children, we are modeling how to respect others *and* teaching them to respect their parents. I believe that if we listen to our children and respond appropriately, even though our teenagers won't always agree with us, they will *respect* us!

● We were having a problem with sarcastic remarks. I even found that my husband and I were being sarcastic at times in our arguing. We made a new family rule. If anyone answered another family member with sarcasm, the one who was the recipient could call out, "Sarcastic." (Other family members could not point it out.) Then the person who made the sarcastic remark would have to do any five-minute job the recipient requested. Any time you make a game out of a problem, it seems to help lessen it.

● When a young child is trying to get my attention, I stop what I'm doing and get down on the child's level to give my full attention.

Some of the best talking times we have had as a family take place when we go out for a sit-down dinner. The phone is far away, and we all seem to be able to concentrate on one another.

12

Cooking, Menu Planning, and Grocery Shopping

~∽⟨∾⟩∽~

The stage of my life when I wrote this chapter was probably not the best time for me to be reflecting on meals and cooking. I was making graduation plans for my oldest son, "doing" baseball season with the other two boys, writing/compiling a book, and besides that, it was the month of May—always frantic and overloaded! Our regular mealtimes flew out the window at that season of the year, since family members typically needed to be in several different locations—all at the same time, of course. Feeling that I could use a good dispatcher at our house about then, I reminded myself that stages of life are temporary. Our dinners those days consisted of hamburgers and hot dogs on the grill, cold-cut sandwiches, pizza, or soup and rolls—anything that could be prepared quickly and easily.

While sitting with one of my sons in the pediatrician's waiting room one time, I picked up a copy of *Gourmet* magazine. After looking at pictures and recipes of pate feuilletee, brioche au chocolat, and stuffed eggs on rosettes with savory sauce, I thought, "Only in my dreams!" Maybe someday I'll have time to make my favorite chicken Parmesan dish or bake that sour cream chocolate cake that I used to bake *before* the kids came along!

Ideas from Other Moms

Cooking

● From the time my children were toddlers, they have *helped* me in the kitchen. I have a picture of my oldest daughter sitting on the kitchen table in training pants with a big bowl of cookie dough between her legs trying to stir with a big wooden spoon. Did it usually take longer to clean up the mess than the time we spent cooking? Yes. Were there days I wondered why I ever asked the question, "Want to help Mommy in the kitchen?" Yes. Do I have great memories of sticky little hands, earnest faces trying to measure ingredients, and, as they got older, surprise breakfasts in bed? Oh, yes. (It was never truly a surprise breakfast. We could hear them banging around in the kitchen, giggling and whispering long before they knocked on our bedroom door. They were always so excited and proud of themselves, and that seemed more important than the mess.) As they reached adolescence, they were able to start dinner if I was running late, and as they leave the nest they are actually competent in the kitchen. It takes time, patience, and a sense of humor to share your kitchen with a toddler, but it pays off in so many ways.

● Our children loved to bake cookies and surprise my husband and me when we came home from an evening out. One daughter proudly presented her cookies (we found egg shells in every bite). After we gently asked about the ingredients, she confidently stated that the recipe called for two *whole* eggs!

● I like Sunday dinner to be special, so no matter what I'm serving, I always set a fancy table the night before. What I like about Sunday dinner is the opportunity to sit around and talk after the meal. We encourage this with our children by serving tea with cream and sugar. From a very early age, they love pouring in the cream and popping in the sugar cubes. This helps minimize afterdinner fidgets!

- Only one bit of advice on kids and cooking: leave the kitchen! Then you won't go crazy watching a mess being made, and your departure will keep you from squashing their creativity.

- Be creative in cooking for toddlers. They love it when we make animal shapes for their lunch. Peanut butter sandwiches can be cut into the shape of a cat face with licorice whiskers, raisin eyes, a chocolate-chip nose, and a marshmallow collar.

- My college-age daughter has remarked that some students eat the *craziest* stuff, almost like they don't know what's good for them! The sad fact is that many of them probably don't know. She thanked me for serving a variety of interesting, nutritious foods through her growing-up years so that she learned about healthy eating. She said she even takes vegetables of her own accord!

- I often talk about good eating habits and healthy foods with my children. At breakfast recently, all four kids were eating huge bowls of oatmeal. After I told them how healthy oatmeal is, my five-year-old solemnly responded, "Even though it really is *gross*, it's good for us."

- One morning I asked my preschooler to get the eggs out of the refrigerator. Eager to help, he went and opened the door, looked in, and stopped to think. Glancing at me with a puzzled look, he said, "Scrambled or fried?"

- When our boys were about two and three years old, they got up one morning while I was still asleep (Dad had already left for work). Fortunately, I didn't sleep a lot longer; but when I came out into the family room, there were a dozen eggs cracked in a pan, and not one *drop* had spilled on the carpet. (There *were* a few shells in the pan though!) My sons were so proud of themselves. A little longer in my bed and they might have decided to try and cook those eggs. . . . I could hardly get upset since there was no mess. I did learn a lesson about trying to sleep in! After picking out the shells, we had scrambled eggs for breakfast!

Menu Planning

I sit down every Sunday evening and clip and file coupons. I then retrieve my grocery store sales flyers that I have filed during the week. Using my sales flyers, coupons, etc., I make out my menu for the coming week. I never have to go through the hassle of figuring out what's for dinner to-night. I only make one trip to the store each week; preplanning menus and purchases saves us a substantial amount of money.

One of my most dreaded tasks is planning meals and making up a grocery list. The chore has been somewhat relieved by each member of my family planning one meal a week, a well-balanced one at that. It's a good experience for them, a tremendous help to me, and a guarantee of at least one meal a week they will like!

My children make their own lunches for school each morning. We discuss before grocery shopping what they would like for the following week. We make it a rule that they have one item from each of the four food groups.

Instead of telling my kids we are having "leftovers," we have a "smorgasbord" dinner when I need to clean out the refrigerator. The kids pretend we are going to a restaurant. They come up with the name of the eating establishment and make a sign. Setting all the food on the kitchen table cafeteria-style, we use trays or plates, choose our food, and sit at the dining-room table. My kids think it's neat that there are so many choices for dinner. With our busy lifestyle, I serve the leftovers about 50 percent of the time. The other 50 percent of the time, my husband cleans out the refrigerator and discovers new life forms.

● Before I go grocery shopping, I sit down and figure out menus for seven days, especially seven suppers. After eighteen years of doing this, it still is not an easy task! I guess because I love to cook and cannot stand to have the same thing over and over, I like to serve various and creative meals. (I believe that when children are served a variety of meals consistently, they tend to be less fussy eaters.) But, alas, sometimes I'm still stumped on what to serve. Lately the kids have been helping me plan meals, and that's been great.

● There comes a time in every family when nothing that Mom makes for dinner is acceptable to the kids. Either they don't like it, or they are tired of it, or it is not exciting enough. A simple solution is to challenge each child to take on the responsibility of planning and cooking for just one meal. No matter how simple the meal is, everyone will have a new appreciation of the effort Mom exerts for the family.

● I think God gives us situations that help us grow in character and attitude, and as a mother of five children He has given me many! Some of these opportunities I have met well, looking to God for His wisdom and strength, though at other times I have failed badly. One situation occurred when a friend was sick and I offered to take a meal to her family. I didn't have the necessary food items on hand, so I got our five small children (ages two months to six years) ready, which took a while—we didn't do anything quickly back then—and off to the grocery store we went. The grocery store was a challenge in itself those days. I needed two carts—one for the groceries and one for the two or three small children who didn't like to or couldn't walk through the store. Someone was always hanging out the side of the cart, so as I was trying to make sure no one fell out, I had to keep my eyes on my other two who were helping me by pulling the needed items off the shelves and putting them in the cart.

By the time I got home I was already exhausted. Now I had to make the meal and get it to my friend's place by 5:00. I fed the children lunch, nursed the baby, and read them their nap story. A few went to sleep, others didn't want to, the baby was fussy, those who went to sleep woke up, those who didn't sleep were crabby, and I tried to make the meal. Finally at 4:50 the meal was made! I had ten minutes to zip it over to my friend's house. I put all the winter coats and hats on again, scooped the baby into her car seat, strapped the toddler into his car seat, and secured the other three with their seat belts. Then I loaded the food into the car. Just as I was pulling out of the driveway, I realized that I had forgotten the card I had purchased for my friend. I turned off the car, ran back to the house, signed the card, and ran back outside.

When I opened the car door, two of my children were crying. I looked at the first one who had been in the front but was now standing on the floor of the back seat. His coat was covered with my casserole. He had taken off his seat belt and flipped over the seat to visit his brother, landing right in the middle of the casserole, which was not only all over him but all over the floor of the car. My second son had stepped right into the brownies with one foot and into the Jello with the other. He had crawled back in his seat, so I had cherry Jello and chocolate brownies all over the seats. I wish I could say I didn't cry!

In my weariness, I stepped back for a moment and asked God for the patience I needed to take care of the meal, the children, and the cleanup. Fortunately, I had made two of some of the food items, intending to use them for *our* dinner. I called my friend and arrived late with a smaller than planned dinner—the best I could do. Our family went to Mc-Donald's that night! Today I laugh as I think about this story. It's a reminder to me that God doesn't just give us patience or whatever, but He gives us the opportunity to acquire those characteristics for which we have been praying.

Grocery Shopping

Who would ever think that Thursday night at the grocery store would be considered a night out! Two little boys fourteen months apart made grocery shopping stressful. After a few trips, I decided it would be better to go by myself in the evening when Daddy was home. So Thursday nights became my time alone, and as strange as it may sound, it really was enjoyable. The bonus was having my husband meet me at the door on my return, so I didn't have to carry the groceries in alone!

Before taking my children to the grocery store, we talked about appropriate behavior. Sometimes they looked forward to choosing one treat for good behavior; other days I explained that we couldn't get treats that day, even though I knew they'd be good! This simple effort on my part was something the children could understand and made our shopping trips as pleasant as possible.

I *never* told my kids that the grocery store had bathrooms. I figured if we visited once, they'd always have to go. I never had a problem until my son went on a preschool field trip to an Eagle supermarket. He came home and promptly told me, "Mommy, do you know that grocery stores have *potties*?"

The cereal aisle at the grocery store can be quite a challenge! My kids and I don't always agree on what kinds of cereals to get. I'm a coupon clipper and tend to collect lots of cereal coupons, though I only clip coupons for the cereals I want my kids to eat. Before going to the store, each of my children select two coupons. This seems to give them an opportunity to choose, yet keeps them within the boundaries. It also helps the budget by buying only those cereals for which we have a coupon.

- When grocery shopping, I put my toddler in the large section of the cart. As I select items, I hand them to the child to organize in the cart. Fragile items go into the child seat section.

- Our four children love boxed cereal for breakfasts *and* snacks (lucky me!). In fact, sometimes they all love the same cereal (unlucky me!). From time to time we have had cereal wars at our house—for example, when the girls come down to breakfast to find their favorite cereal eaten up by those boys! Here is my solution: I buy four boxes of the same cereal and put each child's name on the box.

- To eliminate too many extra foods purchased when you bring children along, have each child decide on one special food item. Each time they see something else they want, let them decide whether they want to trade in their first choice for this new one or keep the original.

- When shopping for groceries, my children help me locate all the items on my list. At the check-out lane, the kids unload the cart while I look through my coupons. I let them choose a candy bar and still feel that I come out ahead since the coupons generally save me more money than the cost of the candy bars.

- Sometimes when our daughter visits her grandma, they go to the supermarket together. One of Grandma's favorite places to shop is an Eagle grocery store. Grandma was amused when on one visit our daughter asked if they could go to the *illegal* store again!

- When Chuck was about three years old, I had him with me doing some grocery shopping. This day the clerks were stocking the entire length of the dairy aisle, with all the boxes lined up in the center. I looked ahead and saw a woman about sixty-five years old with her aged mother, using a walker. I checked the other side of the aisle, but there were a couple of other shoppers coming. I leaned over to Chuck sitting in the cart and said, "Let's have good manners and wait for this elderly lady to go by us" as I tucked the cart into a convenient spot. It took her a long time to make it down the aisle with the walker, and Chuck must have perceived it as quite a procession, because as the older lady came up next to us, he said quite clearly, "Thank you, my majesty!"

13

Daughterſ

I enjoyed reading the book *In the Company of Women* by Brenda Hunter, which speaks to many types of relationships that women experience throughout their lives. One of these, foundational to life itself, is that of mother-daughter. I appreciated some of Brenda's thoughts on the significance of this relationship.

> A mother's capacity to be emotionally close to her daughter is no small thing. From this secure attachment flows the ability to trust others and to provide a safe place for our children, to pass on a bedrock sense of emotional security, while training them to speak the language of the heart. The daughter who has a loving and secure connection with her mother carries her high self-esteem, her ability to take risks, her inner confidence well. She goes through life knowing she has a champion since birth—someone who has always been there to hear her out, lift her up and cheer her on. And what a difference that makes.[24]

Having only sons, I am unable to write from my own experience about daughters! But I have a friend, Joanne, who has four daughters and no sons. I taught all four of her girls piano lessons, and they are delightful. I liked what Joanne had to say about being the mother of girls:

> Having four daughters, I should be an expert, but I am far from it! I am in awe of how God created each one so differently. It keeps me humble. Each one is so unique, yet they are all from the same family. One daughter is creative and a perfectionist. Another is a social butterfly. One is studious and an achiever, and still another has a wonderful imagination. I'm still learning that I can't mold them into what *I* want them to be. God has already made them exactly how he wants them with all their different personalities—each one wonderful. I need to accept each with her own uniqueness and encourage and nurture her special talents. What a challenge! They all need to be handled differently. It would be so much easier if they were all the same, but it wouldn't be nearly as interesting!

Ideas from Other Moms

● I made a promise to my daughter several years ago to take her out for a breakfast or lunch date once a month on the date of her birthday. My daughter and I have a secret place we go on that day. The object of this time alone with my daughter has always remained the same: to listen to her with no interruptions! I only ask open-ended questions, and I listen, listen, listen. She seems to enjoy this time alone with me when she doesn't have to compete for air space with her siblings, with whom I do the same. The children have shared some of their most intimate thoughts on these days.

● Because we had only one child for five years, she was accustomed to being the center of our attention. Shortly before her brother was born, we read a book by Russell Hoban entitled *Best Friends for Frances*, in which Frances and her sister decide to have an all-girls outing without the boy next door. When our son was born, my daughter and I decided to have all-girls outings to keep our special relationship alive. Once a week during the first couple of years of my son's life, she and I left to do something together without the "boys" (my husband and son). My daughter is now twenty-one, and we still have all-girls outings!

- On some evenings when my husband and son are gone, my daughter and I have "Lady Night." We soak in a long, warm bubble bath, and when we get out, we paint our nails!

- My oldest daughter is almost ready to begin menstruation. I've been saving booklets, sample products, and various other little "feminine" items and placing them in a box under my bed. When my daughter's menses starts, I want to give her this box and celebrate her start into womanhood by taking her out to lunch.

- Once or twice a year I plan a getaway with my young daughter. We reserve a room at a local hotel for Friday night, go out for dinner, and plan a morning of shopping on Saturday.

- Having three daughters—two teens and one preteen, I take seriously my role in shaping their views on men, marriage, homemaking, child-raising, femininity, beauty, and purity. Frank and open discussions are important, and we have them; but I also realize how much their attitudes on these issues are "caught" through their observations of myself and other women role models.

- Last semester my young daughter and I took a course at the park district together. We learned how to do sign language, and it was a great way to have a date together each week.

- It's important to have the "big talk" about adolescence and human development *before* a girl's body begins to change— so she is informed, aware, and not frightened. Whether we decide to have a special overnight away or some other special time together, the main thing is to establish open lines of communication, so that as questions arise, the girls feel free to talk to us. My mom did an excellent job in this area with me, and I want to do that for my girls too!

● The women in my husband's family get together every three months to go out to lunch together. This is something my daughter and I really enjoy doing along with the more extended women relations.

● Some of the do's and don'ts on mother-daughter communication that I learned from my mom and practice with my daughters are:

Do:
- *Do be available.* Often the time won't be convenient, but try not to show it.
- *Do be encouraging.* So many people and situations discourage our children. Let them know you're behind them.
- *Do be interested.* They'll never relate to our world until we've learned to relate to theirs.
- *Do be observant.* Know your daughter well. A lot of communication can be nonverbal. Be sensitive to where she is today.
- *Do be understanding.* Look at your daughter's world and the world at large through her eyes.

Don't:
- *Don't be inappropriately angry.* When we display our anger in an unhealthy way, the light switch seems to turn off quickly. Communication has ended.
- *Don't be exasperating.* We need to have realistic expectations for our daughter.
- *Don't be impatient.* Growing into adulthood is hard work and takes time, with many trials and errors along the way.
- *Don't be obnoxious.* If our children are not responding to our discipline, we need to find another and better way to

encourage better behavior or thought. Don't let walls build up between you and your daughter.

- *Don't be unyielding.* Sometimes we are wrong as moms, or we react inappropriately. Don't be afraid to confess your errors.

Several years ago my daughter and I had an *unusual* bonding experience. While I was vacuuming the carpet in our house, my four-year-old daughter Katie decided she wanted to stay close to me, so she followed me around the house as I vacuumed. When I came to the bathroom, she proceeded to lie down at the doorway to the bedroom, which is adjacent to the bathroom. As I backed out of the bathroom vacuuming, she rolled right into the path of the vacuum cleaner, and her long, blonde hair was instantly sucked into the cleaner. She *screamed!* I immediately turned off the machine and tried to get her hair out. It wouldn't budge, since it was totally wrapped around the beater brush on the bottom. I sat there for a couple minutes trying to soothe her and wondering whether I should call 911 or the vacuum repair man. I opted for 911.

Well, the fire truck came, along with the police and paramedics (standard procedure for a call like this). It was quite a scene! They took the vacuum cleaner apart and got my daughter's hair out. It was pretty tangled, and she lost a little hair, but all in all, she was OK. The paramedics turned out to be the right ones to call.

When Katie was in first grade, she wrote about this incident, and her story won first prize in a story contest for kindergartners through second graders. Eventually it was made into a play by the Child's Play Touring Theatre group and was performed at our school. So you see, good things can happen even when it doesn't seem like it during a stressful situation. Be careful what you vacuum!

I enjoy my girls so much! I want the closeness we enjoy now to extend right until the time I die; to accomplish that, I want to build a good foundation. When Daddy (their best buddy) is out of town or working late, my daughters and I often have popcorn parties and watch some type of silly, romantic, musical movie—one he probably wouldn't enjoy watching.

14

Discipline

Discipline your son, and he will give you peace;
he will bring delight to your soul.
PROVERBS 29:17, NIV

For many people, the word *discipline* conjures up the idea of punishment—a spanking, time out in a chair, or having privileges taken away. Discipline may include some of those elements at times, but the term is not synonymous with punishment. It's not a reaction to something a child did or didn't do; it's a think-ahead approach to teaching that produces healthy character and behavior in a child.

Looking back, my husband and I can sure see the positive fruits of early discipline in our sons' lives. They are not perfect, but they are enjoyable to be around. When Jim Dobson authored *Dare to Discipline* over twenty-five years ago, he wrote about the need for balance between love and control. Ecclesiastes 7:18 (NIV) speaks of the need for balance in all of life: "The man who fears God will avoid all extremes."

Going toward the extreme of love with little or no control, allowing the child to run all over parents' authority, ignores the mother's respect for herself. Going toward the extreme of control with little or no love reveals a lack of respect for the child. Either extreme is a lose-lose situation, whereas the proper balance of love and control allows both mother and child to win and encourages mutual respect.

Ideas from Other Moms

● When it comes to discipline, I think consistency is the key word, though that is easier said than done. Life has gone much more smoothly when I disciplined in a consistent manner than when I disciplined only when I was "in the mood." A friend was encouraging to me in this area when my children were young, for which I am thankful.

● I have a friend, Marie-Claire, who said, "People can say as much as they want about discipline and not letting children 'get away' with things. But there are times, at night, when they may be misbehaving out of sheer tiredness, and it's just time to gently take their hand and quietly lead them to bed." And I've found that she's right.

● When our middle son was three, he threw a whopper of a temper tantrum one day in the middle of the kitchen floor. He had asked for something, I had said no, and he decided to put on a grandiose display of kicking and screaming while he was lying on the floor. I was so amazed that I was dumbfounded. After a few seconds I had an urge to do something unconventional. Lying down on the kitchen floor next to him, *I* began kicking. He stopped *instantly*, sat up, and looked at me as though I were out of my mind. We both had a good laugh, and that was the last tantrum I saw.

- I like to discipline with Scripture. It shows my kids that I'm not inventing the rules. Scripture slows the child down and reminds us of God's standards.

- Say what you mean and mean what you say. Always state expectations in advance.

  My husband and I are firm believers in using consequences as part of teaching discipline. In order for this to work, we need to know our child. Spanking our firstborn did not bring about a positive change in her behavior. Yet, if we took away a privilege (such as having a friend over, ice cream, or a favorite video) in response to a wrongdoing, there was successful behavioral change. It was also beneficial for us to link the wrongdoing with the lost privilege. For example, if a friend was wronged, there would be no privilege of having a friend over the next day.

- A friend of mine said she had *one* household rule: *Don't make Mom worry!* It's surprising how many rules fall under this one.

- I whisper when I feel like screaming. It makes the kids aware that I mean business and gives me more self-control. And besides, it saves the neighbors' ears!

15

The Doctor's Office

With Thanks to Kathy Stefo, R.N., B.S.N., L.C.

*I*s my child's fever dangerous? What if this isn't "just a cold"? Is this illness contagious? These are a few of the questions that Kathy hears from parents at least once a day as a pediatrician's nurse. With Kathy's answers to these and other questions, you will be well prepared to handle some of the concerns that surface about your child's health.

How Do I Choose a Doctor for My Child?

For many years parents depended on a pediatrician to care for their children. (A pediatrician is an M.D. with extra training and experience in the care of children under the age of eighteen. A family practice doctor, on the other hand, is an M.D. with broad, less specific training who sees patients of all ages.) Due to changing times in medicine, some insurance companies now require parents to choose a primary care doctor. Before choosing a doctor for your child, check with your insurance company.

Questions you may want to ask a doctor about his services include:

- What type of practice? Private? Group?
- Size of practice? How many doctors in the group?
- How many patients does the doctor schedule per hour?
- How often is the doctor on call?
- Does the doctor have a physician's assistant? If yes, how is he or she used?
- Does the doctor have nurses? How many? Aides? Receptionist?
- Does the doctor do any testing in the office?
- What hospital does the doctor work in and admit patients to?
- Is the doctor board-certified?
- Who answers questions when you call in?
- Who calls back, and how soon?
- What are the doctor's hours in the office? Does he or she have evening or weekend hours?
- What is the fee schedule for visits?
- Does the doctor have more than one office?
- How many sick child openings are left open to be filled by same-day need for appointments?
- How are prescription refills handled?
- Who covers the doctor's patients when he or she is on vacation?

What Should I Expect When I Call the Doctor's Office with a Question?

Rarely will you get to talk to the doctor, since physicians are usually busy seeing patients, though they might return a phone call afterhours for a more serious or chronic problem.

Some offices have receptionists who give your question to a nurse, who then talks to a doctor. Then the nurse calls you back. Most nurses try to get back to patients within a couple of hours.

When you talk to a nurse, she may:

- Schedule an appointment.
- Ask the doctor a question for you.
- Refer you to Billing or the receptionist.
- Check your child's chart for information you need, such as immunizations.
- Take requests for refills.
- Answer questions about physicals.
- Give advice.

Many of you have spent ten, fifteen, or twenty minutes waiting to talk to a nurse, physician's assistant, or doctor. Sometimes the phone nurses are not available, and you connect with the receptionist. Sometimes there's a charge for speaking with the phone nurse or doctor. Sometimes there are long waits for return calls. In order to maximize the time you spend on the phone with your doctor's office or clinic, here are some observations to make and write down *before* you call:

What main things have changed? Behavior? Appearance? Temperature? Bowel movements? Appetite? Pain level? Coughing or wheezing? Have there been recent immunizations or medication changes?

If your child is old enough, ask him or her what hurts. Have them use their hands to show you.

Does the child have a fever? Take the child's temperature, and report how you took it.

Take off most of the infant or young child's clothing to look for any visual body changes. What's swollen? Where's the rash? What does it look like—dry, scaly, red, pink, raised, flat?

Did the child drink or eat any poisons? (Have the bottle at hand if possible.)

If the child is having *a chronic or intermittent problem* such as headaches, diarrhea, allergies, or constipation, note:

- When the problem happened or happens.
- How long it lasted.
- How many times it occurred.
- How severe the situation or pain is. (On a scale of 1 to 10, 1 is little pain, and 10 is agony.)
- Any event or food that triggers the problem.
- What medication your child is taking—prescription name, strength, and number of doses.

Older kids can keep their own calendar or write notes about their day, if necessary. Remember to mention if your child has any preexisting conditions such as asthma.

What If My Child Develops a Fever?

Eighty percent of the phone calls Kathy receives about a sick child involve a fever, and many parents and caretakers react fearfully when their child has one. She often spends a few minutes explaining what an elevated temperature really is, because an explanation arms the parent with a more appreciative view of fevers. When a microorganism, bacterial or viral, invades the body, the body begins a defense to protect itself. An elevated temperature is one of those defenses. As the body produces more white blood cells, the body's metabolism increases, and the temperature begins to rise. Breathing and heart rates also go up. It has been discovered that certain "bad" microorganisms or invaders die more quickly if the temperature of the body rises; so fevers are a sign that your child's immune system is in action.

Bringing a fever down can actually do more harm than good. Studies suggest that a fever *increases* the effectiveness of our microorganism fighters and also improves the effect of some antibiotics! Why are we so afraid? Most parents treat fevers out of fear of febrile seizures and brain damage. The truth is that only a small percentage of children under five years old have seizures with fevers, and these seizures are usually harmless, though frightening.

Most fevers are caused by viral illnesses. When your child has a fever at the beginning of a cold, that's usually normal. If after a few days of a cold they develop a fever, have the child checked for a secondary infection (ear infection, bronchitis, etc.). Age is an important factor in deciding what to do. An infant has an immature immune system and needs to see a doctor if he or she has a rectal temperature of greater than 100.4° F.

If parents view a fever as a possible ally, they will realize that not all fevers need to be medicated away. If your child has a low fever, 99–101°, and is comfortable, he or she doesn't need a fever-reducing medication. Reducing the fever won't make the underlying illness go away any quicker. Also, realize that it is *normal* for fevers to fluctuate during the day. They are usually lower in the morning, rise during the day, and are typically highest in the evenings. With this fact in mind, parents can and should check their child's temperature in the afternoon and before bed to decide if the child should go to school the next day. A temperature then of over 100° should indicate that a child stays home—*not* the morning temperature! Normal morning temperatures mean little as an indicator of whether or not the child will have a fever later in the day. This method is especially helpful for working parents who need time to set up alternate child care or work plans.

When Is a Fever Dangerous?

If your child appears very limp, has rapid breathing or poor coloring, is under a month old with a rectal temperature of over 100°, or is an older child with a fever of 105°, he or she needs rapid medical attention. A rapidly rising temperature can bring on a febrile seizure, as can a high temperature of 104–105°. A febrile seizure is usually not damaging but should not be ignored. Call the doctor, emergency room, or urgent care. While waiting:

- Remove most of the child's clothes or covers.
- If the temperature is over 104° F, put cool cloths or ice packs under the arms and on the groin, or give a tepid water bath (never use alcohol to sponge a child off).
- Give the child cold liquids to drink.
- Many doctors recommend Tylenol or Ibuprofen for fever, but check with your doctor's office (don't use aspirin).

When you report your child's temperature, do not interpret your finding. Just tell the doctor's office the temperature and how you took it.

What If My Child Is Really Afraid or Fights During a Physical Examination?

The best way a mom can help her child through physicals is to be emotionally supportive. Unfortunately, that isn't always as easy as it sounds. It's difficult for us moms to see our children act out their fears or be out of control in front of other adults. Here are a few facts and tips to help you be more supportive at the difficult times:

- Realize that *most* kids act fearful or resistant and need support. Your child isn't the only one.
- Yelling won't help, but calm, firm assistance helps a lot.
- Promising rewards can be helpful, but whispering or screaming threats doesn't help.

- Don't bring other children along—especially when the patient is five or older.
- Nurses don't mind the yelling and crying; it's the physical fighting that gets difficult.
- If your child is extremely afraid, discuss with the nurse how you can help. For injections, it's helpful to have the fearful child lovingly restrained by the parent; no judgments or threats—just a firm, loving hug that helps the child stay still.
- Don't give false praise. If the child acts up, don't say, "My, you were brave!" It's better to say, "I'll bet you're glad that's over!" Of course, it's good to remind them that the medicine keeps bad illnesses from making them terribly sick. Remind them that you love them too!
- Don't compare how one child reacts with another. Each child needs to learn how he or she will cope with pain and fear. Watch your child to see how you can help that child learn a way to cope that works for him or her.

What Are the Generally Recommended Ages for Children's Physical Exams?

1 week	18 months
1 month	2 years
2 months	5 years
4 months	10 years
6 months	14 years
9 months	18 years
12 months	

Many schools demand a sports physical either yearly or every other year, depending on the sport and on school policies.

How Do I Know When to Send My Child to School and When to Keep Him or Her Home?

If the temperature the night before was over 100.4°, don't send the child to school. Wait until they are fever-free for twenty-four hours.

If a rash is draining, spreading, or pimple-like with a clear blister, don't send the child to school; call the doctor.

If a sore throat is accompanied with fever, foul-smelling breath, or a red throat, don't send the child to school; call the doctor.

Do not send the child to school if the child has vomited in the last six hours.

If there have been loose stools more than six times in the last twenty-four hours, or if things are not under control, the child should stay home.

If there is frequent, painful, or bloody urination, keep the child home; call the doctor.

In the event of a severe headache or severe abdominal pain, keep the child home; call the doctor.

16

Education

❧

*O*ur three sons each had positive experiences as students in their elementary, middle, and high schools, and we are grateful for the administrators, teachers, and staff who made significant contributions to their education. Because I respect the principals my children had, Dr. Joan Vydra (elementary), Dennis Rosy (middle school), and Dr. Attila Weninger (high school), I asked all three if I could draw on their experience and expertise for this chapter.

I am grateful for the answers Joan, Dennis, and Attila gave me to the following question: From your experience as an educator, how do you think a mom can best contribute to the success of her child's education and/or schooling? Their comments fell into five sections: (1) building confidence, (2) modeling lifelong learning, (3) enriching your child's life, (4) getting involved, and (5) modeling healthy communication. Under each of these sections are listed specific ideas, some of which are labeled according to age, but many of which are appropriate for all ages.

Build Up the Child's Confidence

One of the most important attributes for success in school and in life is a strong belief in one's abilities. Children who believe they can accomplish high goals will accomplish much more than others. An old adage applies here: If you think you can or if you think you can't, you're right! Those parents who understand the importance of making their children feel special do so in ways that promote strength rather than egotism.

- Send notes in lunches with words of encouragement and praise.
- Set realistic and achievable goals related to school success.
- Encourage a good start to their day at breakfast. If there are upsets on the home front, the student's moods are negatively affected. Prepare them with a positive attitude.
- *Never* make comparisons (positive or negative) with other children.
- Hold up models of genuinely decent people, and guide your children through their tough times with high spiritual goals in mind.
- *Never* criticize before praising.
- Don't put too much pressure on kids about grades in middle school. These are years for nurturing, encouraging, and helping students discover tools for learning and studying.
- Focus on what is achieved rather than what is not achieved. Be supportive of their efforts (regardless of the outcome) in schoolwork, activities, and personal interests.

   We do students a great injustice if we ask them for perfection. We weren't and aren't perfect, and they can't be perfect either. Some parents are concerned when their children receive any grade lower than an A, and that's not healthy.
- Spend quality time with your children every day.
- Tell them about, show, offer, and create opportunities for them to succeed.

Model Lifelong Learning

Parents are their children's best teachers. Most children would rather emulate their parents than anyone else; so if parents want their children to become passionate and lifelong learners, they must model those behaviors for their children. This means that parents should be reading a mix of fiction and non-fiction books, as well as newspapers and trade journals. When questions come up about something to which an answer is not readily apparent, parents can say, "Let's go find the answer in our encyclopedia" or, these days, look it up on CD-ROM. Parents can also take a class here and there in an area of interest or even show a willingness to become self-taught, learning something new and different. What is important is that parents show that they are continually stretching, growing, and learning new things.

Enrich Your Child's Life

Educators have learned a great deal in the last few years about cognition, including the fact that children who are immersed in rich learning experiences have a much easier time learning in school. Those children who have been exposed to museums and theaters, to zoos and historical sites, bring those experiences with them to the literature they read, to the facts they find in textbooks, and even to the conversations they have in their classrooms. Here are some things you can do *together* to enrich your child's life:

- Visit museums and cultural centers.
- Visit farms, zoos, and factories that allow tours.
- Visit shopping malls.
- Visit libraries, including those in other towns and cities.
- Visit historical sites and then follow up by reading about that history.

- Choose ethnic restaurants instead of just the tried and true "American" fare.
- Visit county and state fairs.
- Monitor what your child watches on TV, taking advantage of learning channels.
- Go on trips to different areas of the country, soaking up the traditions.
- Go on trips to different geographic regions, noting the different landforms.
- Expose your child to great art, literature, and music.

Get Involved

Children are far more likely to be successful in school if their parents are involved in their education. This involvement should take place on several different levels.

- Talk with your children each and every day about school.
- Especially in the elementary grades, talk with your children each day about completed work.
- Read to your young children at least fifteen minutes each day.
- Help drill spelling words, math flash cards, or whatever else needs to be learned.
- Volunteer to help in your children's elementary classroom, weekly if possible.
- Join the PTA, and help with PTA events as often as possible.
- Learn about technology, and assist your child in that learning.
- Ask children questions about school, friends, and activities. Even if you are met with resistance as they get older, continue to let them know you are interested.
- Don't take a hands-off policy when they get to middle school. Even though the apron strings are beginning to be cut, parents should continue to work together with the school.

Model Healthy Communication

- Let your children's school and teachers know how much you appreciate their efforts, then watch how much harder they work to keep pleasing you.
- If a student receives a poor grade, approach the issue calmly, with questions: What's happening in this class? Is that your best work? Is there some way I can help you improve?
- Be supportive by listening and encouraging.
- If you have questions about the way things are being handled, don't go on the offensive. You will get farther faster if you begin by seeking information. When approaching the school, always talk to the teacher first. Aim to develop mutual understanding and relationships with your child's teachers.

Another educator who contributed to this section is Joan Darnauer, a fifth grade teacher from Goodland, Kansas. I wanted a teacher's perspective on how moms can best work with their children's teachers. She shared six thoughts:

- The more the parent communicates with the teacher, the better idea the teacher will have of who the child really is. The teacher will begin to see glimpses of the child through the parent's loving eyes.
- The stronger the trust between parent and teacher, the better the situation for the student.
- Let teachers know how much they are appreciated— especially when it's not the holidays!
- Tell the teachers right at the beginning that you support them and want to work with them as allies. Kids too need to know there's a united front between parent and teacher. Even if there's a value difference, the child needs to know that the parent respects the position and authority of the teacher.

- Even though homework is a child's responsibility, parents can offer *accountability*, which is greatly encouraging to teachers.
- For a child who's not a fast learner, parents are wise to supplement in areas of weakness. Extra time may need to be set aside for things like math facts or spelling words.

Ideas from Other Moms

Mornings

My suggestions for getting ready for school in the morning are short, but they seem to work at our house. The more we set out and get done the night before, the more smoothly our mornings seem to go. I set the breakfast table. The children lay out their clothes and place their backpacks down by the back door. Books, instruments, posters, projects, or whatever they may need are taken to the door. At night we talk about the time schedule for the next morning so we all know what to expect. The most important thing we do is to pray with our children before they leave for school. That seems to help them meet their day with a sense of security and love.

Before my daughter started kindergarten, she and I discussed the idea that she would need to get up at the same time every school morning. I offered her two choices: we wake you up every morning, or we give you your own alarm clock. She chose to have her own alarm clock. She is now in high school and continues to set her alarm and get up on her own every school morning. Not only has she learned to take responsibility for her schedule, but any tension between parent and child regarding getting up has been diffused. The alarm clock is the only bad guy.

Since my kids attend different schools and leave in the morning at staggered times, it's a great chance for me to focus on each child individually. The last child to leave naturally gets the most attention. That hour together is a great time to read, finish homework, work on projects, practice spelling words, practice piano, or clean pet cages together.

One morning we timed how long it took to pull up the sheets on the girls' beds, throw the pillows in place, pull up the comforters, and put the pillow shams at the top of the beds. It was less than a minute. That was the end of the "I didn't have time to make my bed" excuse. They had to make their beds and get dressed before coming to the kitchen for breakfast. I felt that gave them some responsibility and was that many less beds for me to worry about. I must confess that after we moved to a two-story home where I sometimes didn't get back upstairs until later in the day and the kids were teenagers, I found unmade beds and clothes on the floor. At that point I had to decide how big a priority a neat room is, because teens don't seem to even notice the mess. I live with the hope that they will become neat adults and remember Mom's words of wisdom: "The whole room seems neater just by making the bed."

Morning rushes go more smoothly if there is organization the night before. Lay out all clothing, including shoes. Check to be sure all library books and homework are in backpacks. Lunches can be made and put in the refrigerator, sandwiches made and frozen, even up to a week ahead of time. Backpacks, jackets, and shoes should be by the exit door.

On our kitchen counter is a candy jar with a sign on the front that reads: "You may have a piece of candy if you:

- Ate your breakfast.
- Brushed your teeth.
- Made your bed.
- Read your Bible.
- Tidied your room.
- Are ready to leave by 8:45.

Since I take a little while to wake up in the morning, I plan breakfast and sometimes even set the table before I go to bed, so that everything is ready in the morning. When the children were little, we discussed at bedtime what the weather was going to be the next day and planned clothing that would be appropriate. I always gave them a choice within broad parameters of what they wanted to wear.

Homework

We are flexible when it comes to homework. We don't demand that it be done prior to playing, etc. We find that our kids respond to making wise choices. Many times their attitude is better if they're allowed to play first and blow off a little steam. Sometimes it pays off to get out of the school mode and return to it later on. If the kids make the choice to put off homework and it doesn't get done, they pay the consequence the next day: homework first and no playing—period.

Homework and weekends do not seem to go together. We strongly encourage our daughter to complete her homework as early as possible on the weekend. She has seen the value of being able to relax or do things with friends the rest of the weekend, avoiding the pressure of staying up late on Sunday night to hurriedly finish homework. She often does homework on Friday nights while baby-sitting. The same "early on" policy applies to holiday breaks.

We have always tried to be available for homework help. I have actually liked algebra this time around! I guess the trick has been learning along with them and communicating how enjoyable that has been.

The rule in our household has always been homework first, and it has been enforced since day one. The boys know that once they are home, they are to complete their homework before doing anything else. I think afterschool activities have been helpful; when they get home, they have already had time to unwind and are ready to get to work. Involvement in community theater, music lessons, Scouts, and sports has helped them learn time management skills so they can participate in these desired activities. They have learned that planning ahead (e.g., working ahead on weekends) will make the weekdays go much more smoothly for them, especially during times of peak involvement in sports or theater activities.

My friend June received a call from her son's teacher (who one year was chosen as the Minnesota Teacher of the Year). She asked if June had been helping her son with his homework. June said she did look his homework over and then would suggest that he might want to take another look at, say, problem #5. He'd look it over, realize his mistake, and then fix it. The teacher mentioned that she saw a difference between the quality of his *school*work and his *home*work, and she felt that the quality of his *school*work would improve if he stopped doing so well on his *home*work. June agreed to back off at home. When she did, his grade dipped slightly, but he eventually was motivated to pull it back up. Of course, a parent needs to be balanced in using this approach. Sometimes we do need to help kids with homework, but not to the point that they fail to face up to the real picture of their abilities or the need for clarification of something they don't understand.

I really can't claim that I have a homework system that works well—it's an area we're striving to improve. But I do have a story! In Judd's elementary school when a student has not finished a homework assignment, he or she receives a purple slip. When the student gets a third purple slip in one trimester, he or she receives a detention and has to stay after school. At one point Judd already had two slips, and I was more worried about him receiving a detention than he

118

was, because *I* was the one who would be inconvenienced by having to make arrangements for him to be picked up after school while I would be heading for work.

I spoke with a wise friend. Her comment was to make the detention inconvenient for *him*. She suggested that I say something like, "Hey, Judd, you know, if you get another purple slip, you'll have to stay late at school and you'll miss the bus home. You also know that I will be working that afternoon and won't be able to pick you up. So I was wondering what arrangements you would make if you have to stay late? I'm guessing that Aunt Esther might be willing to pick you up, but I just wondered if you'd have the $3 she'd probably need to charge you for her time, gas, and inconvenience."

In other words, put the ball in his court—a kind of "tough love." There's much more motivation not to let this happen if his wallet is hit. As I recall, I made a statement to Judd similar to the one above, and he did become motivated to avoid that third purple slip.

● For our child with attention deficit disorder, we have found it extremely helpful to have a private tutor. We schedule the tutor for the heaviest homework evening or morning. This relieves a lot of pressure from the family *and* the child, plus it gives our child another source of support and information.

School

● Instead of asking a child, "How was school today?" ("Fine") and "What did you do in school today?" ("Nothing"), encourage discussion by asking, "What was one good thing or bad thing that happened in school today?"

● Getting to know the teachers of our children is extremely important and time well spent. As a child, my grade school teachers were invited to our home for lunch a few times during the year. It was a wonderful time to get to know each other on an informal basis and a special time for me as a child. I have tried to do similar things for the teachers of my children. Volunteering in the classroom, giving little gifts and remembrances at times other than the holidays, thank-you notes, and phone calls all let the teacher know that we appreciate the time and effort spent with our children. I try not to forget the principals, librarians, secretaries, etc. They are also a part of my children's daily lives, and I like getting to know them as well. In the older grades in which there are multiple teachers, a Christmas card with a picture of the family and a personal note can help the teacher associate that child with his family and is thus much appreciated.

• About once a week I walk into the school building to pick up my elementary school children at the end of the day. This helps me build a better relationship with the teachers and school staff and provides an opportunity for their teachers and me to interact, even if there is only time for a smile and a kind word. Teachers often have topics, ideas, anecdotes, and concerns they are eager to share informally, and it helps me develop a better appreciation for their job. Without these informal meetings I am sure that communication would be limited to issues they and I felt were monumental enough to require a phone call or note home. These brief appearances also give me the opportunity to catch a candid glimpse of my sons with their classmates and to assess the school atmosphere.

• Place an afterschool snack on the table when children come home. They are then more willing to share about their day. The snack is an incentive to sit and talk.

• We have chosen to homeschool our two daughters. Our reasons for beginning ten and a half years ago are different from our reasons for continuing today. When we began, we felt that our children needed to be with us longer; they needed instruction in Christian character and the mature examples we could give them. We homeschool now because it works for us. Academically, our girls are doing extremely well. Our schooling gives them time for extra piano practice—especially our oldest who is working toward a career in music. They can be involved in projects, service, and ministry at times of day that a traditional school would render impossible. We enjoy our winter out-of-town company without having school and carry on when they leave, catching up in the spring, if necessary. We are blessed to be part of a large (450-plus families) homeschooling school. This has brought our family closer together in every way.

- Periodically send notes to teachers from you or your child. They need reminders of support and words of encouragement at times other than just Christmas and Teacher Appreciation Day.

- Because I work in the local high school, my friends who are parents of students at my school often come to me with their "teacher" concerns. I guess I am particularly sensitive to teachers since I have been a teacher and have worked with teachers. I feel that if a parent has a concern with a teacher, the first step should always be to go to that teacher via phone, note, or school visit to discuss the problem. Begin by saying something positive about the class. Be honest in your assessment of the situation. Be reasonable and pleasant. Teachers are people too—people who work hard, sometimes teaching 150 students a day. If a parent feels the problem cannot be resolved with the teacher, then the parent should go to the department chair. After these two avenues of pursuit, the parent may wish to contact the assistant principal or the head principal. But it's always best to begin with the teacher.

- When my children were in grade school, I tried to be around school enough to know their teachers. We were fortunate to have positive experiences through most grades, but being aware of the teacher and the classroom situations always benefited our children. One year my daughter had a teacher who seemed less than dedicated to teaching and was often harsh with the children. However, knowing that her little grandson was dying of leukemia helped me to have patience with her and to teach my daughter compassion for others. We prayed for the teacher's family and learned some good life lessons in third grade. Sometimes helping our children means not removing them from a tough situation or protecting them from hurt as much as teaching them how to handle the tough stuff that happens to each of us.

At the end of each year, we had a Teachers' Appreciation Lunch at our home for our children's teachers just to say thank you. We fussed over the invitations and fixed something fun to eat, concentrating on making the teachers feel special that day. The kids loved it, and each year the teachers seemed to look forward to it also.

Every year at Thanksgiving, I take coffee cakes to the school offices where each of my children attend and send packages of homemade cookies to each teacher. (Some years this has included as many as eighteen different teachers!) Along with the goodies, I write notes of appreciation, thanking each one for their contribution to the education of my child. Through the years, my concerns have been few, but whenever I have voiced them they have been taken seriously because I don't have a reputation for complaining—I have a reputation for affirming.

My kids loved it when I volunteered at their schools. Being a room mom or sports mom helped me get to know other moms, the teachers, and the classmates of my children. This continues in high school and college. Even soccer players in college love cookies after a game!

● Since time is our most precious commodity, we have found that volunteering in activities in which our children are directly involved is the best use of our volunteering time. In grade school, we volunteered in the child's classroom and in school-related activities. This is without a doubt the best way to stay in touch with our children's school activities and their teachers, gaining information about how the school functions. As the children got older, we volunteered in band, art, and sports activities as well. We found that the more involved we were, the more committed our children were, and the more they achieved in that activity. It became a family activity instead of something at which the children were dropped off each week.

Having teenagers now, we can look back and fine-tune decisions made in earlier years. One of those "if I had to do it over again" decisions would be to sit down with each child and decide as a family what that child's activities would be for the year and then have at least one of the parents involved in the activity with the child whenever possible. Quality always seems to be better than quantity.

● When our oldest son started first grade, he was a baseball score-aholic. All summer long he daily checked scores of all the previous day's games. To make his transition to lunch at school easier, I wrote down the scores of some of his favorite teams on his napkin. He looked forward to lunch, and all his buddies at his table couldn't wait to see the scores. This occurred through the football and basketball seasons as well.

● Be sure to include volunteer work for school, church, or wherever on your child's resumé. We develop a lot of our gifts in these settings!

● I think that volunteering at school and within the community is valuable. Having a presence in the school is important. While we may not agree with everything that goes on in a school, being there on a volunteer basis not only attunes us to the school's atmosphere but builds our credibility with the teachers. Then when we have a legitimate complaint or issue to discuss, we have a better chance of being heard.

● I find that volunteering in my child's classroom and school is particularly rewarding. Not only does my child love seeing me there, but I am conveying the value I place on her and her education. The side benefit for me has been getting acquainted with the kids in my child's classroom and, quite often, the moms. The conversation with my daughter is always better when I know who she is talking about. I also feel more comfortable letting her go to a friend's home when I know the friend and the mom.

A word of caution on volunteering: When it starts to negatively impact home life, learn to say no. A stressed-out or often absent mom can cancel out the positives of volunteering.

● A kindergarten student kept crying every time he came to school. One evening he and his mother sat down to talk about the problem. As it turned out, he didn't like saying the Pledge of Allegiance to the American flag. When asked why, he started crying and told his mom that his teacher was talking about witches. Through sobs and tears, he said the Pledge, and when he got to "for which it stands," the words came out, "four witches stand." After the misunderstanding was cleared up, he returned to school a much happier student!

● My five-year-old kindergartner was leafing through the things I had put in his backpack for him to take to school. He came across a note I had written for his teacher. He brought the note over to me and, pointing to the words, exclaimed, "Oh, Mommy, my teacher can't read cursive!"

Vacation Days

Summer vacations from school can be such an enjoyable time. I love having my children home and am not usually eager to see school start again in the fall. After so many months of structure and time restrictions, it is wonderful to relax. Our summers are as unstructured and free from commitments as I can make them—plenty of time to swim, play, read, get together with friends for outings, take a vacation, and yet have a little order to our lives. In order to be free for the kids, I do as little housework as possible and enlist their help so we can play sooner. There is plenty of time when they go back to school to do the big jobs.

My suggestion for vacation days from school is to *not* go where everyone else goes (the children's museum, the science museum, etc.). I personally don't enjoy being at those places when they're supercrowded, which they usually are on vacation days. We enjoy visiting the library on those days or going swimming. One time I mixed some dough in the breadmaker and made animal bread by shaping bits of dough into turtles, snakes, dinosaurs, etc. The end results were cute—and fun to eat!

Our government, and the greeting card industry, recognizes Mother's Day and Father's Day. We decided to institute a "Kids' Day." The first day of summer vacation from school received this "official" designation. We allowed the kids to plan an activity that they thought would be fun for them; then Mom and Dad cleared their calendars to make sure the day was a success.

When the boys were little and I was working, I used to take a vacation day when they were off school, and we went to the zoo with friends, baked cookies, went to a movie, or visited a museum. Now that they are older they look forward to the break in their busy routine and usually want to invite friends over. So I go into work early in the morning in order to be home by noon. While I'm gone, the boys have a list of tasks they must accomplish. These may include homework, writing thank-you notes, vacuuming a room, dusting, brushing the dog, making lunch, etc. I pay them for their work, and they seem to enjoy the sense of accomplishment as they check the items off their individual lists. They also enjoy the extra spending money! I feel better knowing that though home alone for a short time, they have structure to their activities. Then they enjoy spending the afternoon at home with friends.

When the kids get an *unexpected* day off from school (snow day or whatever), most families are usually unprepared. One snow day in February, we spontaneously planned and hosted an early Valentine's Day party for the neighborhood kids. We decorated with crepe paper and made a heart-shaped cake and valentines. The kids loved it, and the other moms were truly grateful!

17

Exercise

Through the years I've tried various forms of exercise: calisthenics in my bedroom in the morning, swimming at a local pool at 6 A.M. (that lasted about a month), aerobic videos, and walking. Some of my attempts have come and gone, but I *have* exercised regularly for about twenty years. Walking/jogging in the nice weather and aerobic videos in the basement during the cold weather are the two varieties that work best for me. Walking with a friend is a great way to connect, although when walking alone I enjoy praying. When I walk/run at the local Wheaton College track, I pray for a different friend or family member each time around.

The biggest challenge is finding a time that works. Each year I reevaluate my schedule and figure out where my exercise routine fits in. When my kids didn't start school until 9 A.M., I met a friend at 6 and walked. Some years were more of a challenge than others.

I'll never be asked to be on the cover of a fitness book, but since I've started exercising consistently, I've felt better, I have plenty of energy, I concentrate better, and it's a good stress buster. Lots of the ideas for this book were formed while I was out walking!

Ideas from Other Moms

● Exercise is good for our bodies, but it's even better for our minds! I try to plan a time and a type of exercise that will always work—rain or shine, whether the kids are healthy or sick, using any part of the day when I have time. I can't always get out to that exercise class, but if I have a plan at home, I'm more likely to be consistent even when the rest of life isn't! Fresh air is great for me and my kids, so I walk whenever I can.

● Last year we joined a health club, partly to make exercise part of the family definition of "fun," rather than "fun" being defined solely as "pizza." It wasn't an easy decision to join because of the expense involved, but we feel we have received our dollars' worth in terms of a healthier lifestyle and fun activities for the *whole* family. I feel that if we can model for our children that taking care of ourselves physically is important, they may learn that pattern now and continue it after they've left the nest. The club even has a "family fitness fun" class that we can all attend together, which involves using a step, mats, scooters, jump ropes, and hula hoops! And we can go swimming indoor all year 'round and outside in the summer.

● As a medical doctor and a mom, I recommend at least twenty minutes of aerobic exercise three times a week. When my children were young, I marched around the house with them. When they learned to ride bikes, I jogged beside them. As they get older, it *does* get easier to make time for exercise!

● Exercise—just do it! I don't wait until I feel like doing it, and I don't give in when I don't feel like doing it. Walking outdoors has been therapeutic for me. I enjoy the fresh air, clear my head, and do my three P's: *pray, plan, and ponder.*

● When I exercise, I either do step aerobics with a video while the kids are asleep, or I use the exercise bicycle while the kids are watching a video.

● When I invest money in exercising, I am more likely to follow through. When I involve another family member or a friend, I am more likely to continue. When I sign my child up for a class at the same time, I am more likely to go for their sake.

● I walk with my neighbor in the evenings after supper. Besides the value of the physical exercise, it's great for talking out our feelings. Women need other women to talk to so we don't wear out our husband's listening ears!

18

Forgiveness

In the church that my family and I are a part of, the congregation repeats the Lord's Prayer and the Apostles' Creed together every Sunday morning. Sometimes repetition causes us to take things for granted or traditions to seem common. Not so for me on this practice. Each Sunday morning I speak aloud my belief that Jesus' blood has provided forgiveness for my own sin, and I'm reminded that if I really believe that truth, it works out in my life as I forgive others—"Forgive us our sins, as we have forgiven those who have sinned against us." There have been weeks that I have stumbled in my heart when I came to those words, knowing that I had not forgiven someone or was having difficulty in the process. I still have a lot to learn about grace and forgiveness, but of this I am sure: as people and events in my life surface and forgiveness becomes necessary, I grow to appreciate the forgiveness Jesus has offered me and the great price that He paid on my behalf—His own life.

I have always loved the story of Joseph in the Old Testament. I have never been able to read or hear that account without getting a lump in my throat. After Joseph experienced the mistreatment of his brothers, separation from his father, and all the hurt and anger that went along with all that, he declared, "As far as I am concerned, God turned into good what you meant for evil, for he brought me to this high position I have today so that I could save the lives of many people" (Gen. 50:20). Sometimes we find ourselves in life situations that feel as if we will *never* recover from loss, pain, betrayal, or grief. When our pain is new and fresh, we do not usually realize that our painful experiences can eventually have redemptive value in our life, and even for those around us. But as healing takes place, we eventually see redemption.

Gil Beers, an author friend of mine, has shared from his heart regarding the sudden death of his twenty-six-year-old son. "Seeds of strength are planted in the soils of weakness. Your most uplifting strength tomorrow may grow from your most debilitating weakness today."[25] It's only because of God's history of forgiveness to mankind and His redemptive activity in my life that I can see my *need* to be forgiven and find His *strength* to forgive another.

Whenever I hear lessons on forgiveness, I'm quick to think of what forgiveness is *not*. It is not ignoring the truth. To the contrary, I am able to forgive only after I have spoken the truth in love to a person who has wronged me. This helps defuse my desire to get even or to give the offender the "silent treatment," neither of which is right. Forgiveness also does not mean saying, "That's okay"; it's *not* okay. Forgiveness is releasing another from our desire to take revenge or get even, choosing rather to look to God to set things straight. And He *always* does, even though it's often not in our way or in our time.

Ideas from Other Moms

● I have blown it many times as a mom. When I have humbled myself and gone to one of my children and asked for forgiveness or prayer, they have responded with love and forgiveness that strengthened our relationship.

It is impossible to live a life free of mistakes. No one, other than the God-man, Jesus, ever has or ever will. Therefore, everyone has something in their past they would change if they could. The point is, we can't change the past. It is important to face it honestly, deal with the hurts and failures, weigh the successes for what they were, and accept responsibility for our own errors without assuming the guilt of others.

Most important, we must learn the lessons God provides along the way. The path to maturity involves evaluating the past, setting goals for the future, and making discerning decisions in the present. No matter what our age when we stop to reflect on our past, we still have tomorrow to consider. So as mothers, if we made mistakes with one child, we don't have to repeat them with the next; or we can become a terrific grandmother to the next generation. Maybe by sharing our mistakes, God will help someone else not to make them.

Another benefit of recognizing our own weaknesses or failures is that we become more accepting and forgiving of others. The Bible commands us to "be kind to one another, tenderhearted, forgiving one other, just as God has forgiven you because you belong to Christ" (Eph. 4:32). We all have regrets, and we can't rewrite history. However, our God is faithful and promises us peace of mind and inner joy when we focus our today and tomorrow on Him.

Years ago I had a friend who told me that she told her children many times each week that she was sorry for many things, big and little. I thought how freeing it must be for her children to be able to come to her with their mistakes and later take them to Christ. I'm sure her children can see Christ living in her. We are our children's main

132

example, bad or good, and I think teaching our children about God's forgiveness through our acts of forgiveness will strengthen their love for Christ and help them understand God's grace.

I recall one time when my daughter, then a young child, made a great connection with scriptural truth. She was probably about seven or eight, and she was struggling with order in her life. I asked her to clean up her bedroom, and after a while she called me to do a room check. I viewed a room that *appeared* to be back in order, but I soon realized that the clutter had merely been pushed under her bed, into her closet, and into her dresser drawers. She was then asked to fold, stack, and properly store everything. Later that night, after tucking her into bed, she called me back into her room. She wanted to pray and ask Jesus to forgive her for her dishonesty. She said, "Mom, my life is kind of like my room. It looks nice on the outside, but inside it is messy because I disobeyed and didn't tell the truth. I'm sorry." What a thrill it was to kneel beside her bed as she asked Jesus to forgive her and make her clean from the inside out!

Boy, forgiveness is a tough one for me. Even when I think I have forgiven, the hurt and the grudge sometimes hang on. I pray a lot, asking God to show me the way to forgive completely. Matthew 7:1-2 (NIV) helps me: "Do not judge, or you too will be judged. For in the same way you judge others, you will be judged, and with the measure you use, it will be measured to you." That's enough to make me want to forgive! I like the next line, too: "Why do you look at the speck of sawdust in your brother's eye and pay no attention to the plank in your own eye?" Man, does that hit home! Try changing the word "brother" to "child." I think this is so important in our role as parents. Over and over we must forgive our children completely and wipe the slate clean. It's too easy to see their faults but forget our own shortcomings.

● Sometimes after yelling at the kids, I'm able to swallow my pride and ask for their forgiveness. I wish I did this more. Other times I ask them to pray for me, and they do—right then. This helps us all to get a better perspective.

● I realize that every human relationship (including mother-child) will disappoint; we all at times fail each other. *Only* God's relationship to us will not. As a result, I see grace as the God-given means to make up the difference of what each relationship lacks. He can fill us with His forgiveness and love. God's grace can sustain every mom to be the woman of God she seeks to become, so that at the end of her parenting, when she reflects on her successes and her failures, her children will rise up and call her blessed and she will sense the abounding grace of God!

19

Friends and Hospitality

Moms need friends. Kids need friends. *Everybody* needs friends! We also have to work carefully at *being* good friends. Not to be confused with an acquaintance, "a person whom we know," a friend is defined as "a person whom we know, like, and trust." Throughout our lives we typically have many acquaintances, but friends require more time and investment—and give great dividends in return. Sharing common values and interests, some of my friends are mothers of my children's friends, some share my love for music, some are friends from college days, and others are neighbors. As a result of time spent together, we build a history of shared experiences, some of which may be lighthearted or hilarious and some of which become precious because of honest transparency.

It's important to me that my close friends share a love for God, His truth, and His righteousness. Proverbs 27:19 reminds us:

> A mirror reflects a man's face, but what he is really
> like is shown by the kinds of friends he chooses.

Choices are important in my friendships with other women, and in my children's friendships as well. There is a lot that children need to be protected from, and I believe it's a mom's responsibility to look out for her young children's relationships. I remember several times when our boys were quite young that we stepped in to offer redirection to a relationship, sometimes realizing more space was necessary. Adults and children ought to have a variety of friends; that makes our lives more interesting and promotes healthy social lives.

Friendships involve both giving and taking. Beware of the relationship where one person is a giver and the other a taker, with roles that never seem to change. That's not a friendship, and it might even be an unhealthy situation. Mutual respect is an important ingredient in the friendships of adults and children alike.

Hospitality in our relationships occurs in so many ways. Warmth and generosity are key here. When we hear the word *hospitality*, we sometimes limit our thoughts to having guests in our home or entertaining others. But we can be hospitable when we're at our child's school. We can exercise hospitality in our car pool or at the grocery store. I believe hospitality is a mind-set coming straight from God's Spirit, and it flows through all of our actions, wherever we may be.

Ideas from Other Moms

Kids and Friends

Friends are important to children from a very early age, and we've always had an open door policy—the more the merrier! The best way to get to know our children's friends is to have them in our home and make them feel welcome. We are probably happiest when our kids are all home and they have brought their friends with them.

● One of my favorite little sayings hangs in our home school-room. It's on a poster, filled with various little faces in all shapes and colors: "Friends come in all flavors." We have had this hanging since our two daughters were preschoolers, because we want them to look at every person, regardless of age, color, or gender, as a potential friend. This doesn't mean we have allowed them to play with anyone that knocked on our front door, indiscriminately and without any boundaries. We have tried to teach them that our friends can help build us up or tear us down, and we must choose carefully. We want them to be friendly to everyone, and not just to their peers. This is something that we as adults often need to relearn in our own lives. Do we exemplify James 2:2–4 (NIV)?

> Suppose a man comes into your meeting wearing a gold ring and fine clothes, and a poor man in shabby clothes also comes in. If you show special attention to the man wearing fine clothes and say, "Here's a good seat for you," but say to the poor man, "You stand there," or, "Sit on the floor by my feet," have you not discriminated among yourselves and become judges with evil thoughts?

● When my children were small and were planning to have friends over, I wanted their time to be as pleasant as possible. Knowing all kids want their friends to do what *they* want to do, I decided to address the potential and probable conflict before it arose. I asked my kids what they wanted to do when their friend came over. When they gave their list of ideas, I said, "That sounds like fun, but what if _____ doesn't want to do that? What if they want to _____?" I felt that talking about the issue ahead of time helped my kids address the needs of a guest, avoid fighting, and learn skills in conflict resolution. It didn't *always* work, but as they get older, I see growth in their kindness and diplomacy.

● Our son, when six, needed to be hospitalized at various times for fever, infection, or other problems associated with battling childhood leukemia. The best surprise we ever gave him the night before surgery was a visit from his best friend. His eyes sparkled, and the smile on his face from ear to ear told us that his need to have the familiar in a place where things were scary had just been met. We couldn't have created a better remedy for an anxious evening.

● I have always prayed for the friends that surround my children. How faithful God has been in providing for them. I have also prayed for my children to be good friends, to stand up for what is right, and to defend others if necessary. They are not perfect, but God has been good in providing balance—friends to whom they need to minister, and friends who minister to them. They have been let down and they let down, but what they are learning is shaping them for the rest of their lives.

● Encourage your children to bring their friends home with them; that's a wonderful way to keep track of what they're doing and what they're talking about. If we listen and observe carefully, we learn how to better encourage them.

● When our kids are going out with their friends, there is a list of questions that they have come to expect from us, their parents. In fact, they have learned that they will receive permission for the activity much more quickly if they plan ahead and have the answers ready. At times when we have forgotten to ask some of the questions, they almost seemed offended that we didn't care! Here's our list:

- Where are you going?
- What are you going to do?
- Who are you going with?
- How are you getting there?
- How are you getting home?
- When will you be home?
- Do their parents know that you are coming over?

- Are their parents going to be there?
- What movie are you going to watch (if applicable)?

Don't be afraid to ask! And don't be afraid to offer an alternate suggestion! They appreciate that we care.

I like to get to the bottom of a frustration and figure out a solution. One problem we were having was Wednesdays. The kids scattered to friends' houses after school and came home at 6 P.M., only to announce that they had homework, and church clubs began at 6:45! In addition, I was frustrated that with four children there was never a time when they were all consistently home together, especially to coordinate weekly chores. I came up with a solution and thought up the catchy name, "Wednesday No Friends Day." The kids all knew not to make plans after school for that day; everyone would be responsible for some cleaning chores; homework was finished before dinner. This solved all the problems in one swoosh.

At first it was hard because other friends were doing things. But once word got out, several of my children's friends' parents started "Wednesday No Friends Day" too; so my kids weren't missing anything. Some Wednesdays we skip the chores and just do a family outing for ice cream or something fun. They don't even miss the old Wednesdays!

Moms and Friends

I have been blessed with great women friends who share many of my same feelings, goals, and desires for their children. We spend a lot of our times together discussing our children. Sometimes we laugh, and sometimes we cry! Some of my closest friends have already gone through many of the same things I am now experiencing, and I depend on them a lot. Since I am a quiet observer, I take mental notes of what seems to work for others and what doesn't. Another reason my friendships are so important is that we take turns watching each other's children!

It can be so difficult to find time for friends, especially for the mother with little ones, but it's so important because *every* mother needs friends to:

- Help keep life in perspective—it's more than diapers and bottles.
- Encourage one another—we learn together.
- Lend a helping hand—often four hands are better than two.
- Share our joys—it makes for twice the fun.
- Share our sorrows—it makes for half the grief.
- Pray for one another—sometimes we can't pray for ourselves.
- Rebuke one another—we all need to be kept in line.
- Learn from each other's mistakes—it can be difficult to know when to keep our mouths shut and when to speak.
- Have fun together—laughter is the best medicine.
- Build memories and grow old together.

When each of my children was born, the women of the church brought in food to help out. I received new recipes, and as a result we have Mrs. Burgess's "Katie's Jello," Mrs. Peterson's "Michael's Pudding Dessert," and Mrs. Govertsen's "Jason's Spaghetti Cheesebake" at our house. Whenever I serve these foods, it is a reminder to my family of the thoughtfulness of friends in the body of Christ when children were born. My children have a greater interest in making and delivering meals to people in our church because of this.

My husband and I have been part of a small group Bible study as long as we've been married (eighteen years). This has provided strength, encouragement, and fun for us. I think it's important for couples to uphold each other in decisions and prayers for us and our children.

Earthly role models are wonderful people who have been through a stage in life that we have yet to conquer and who seem to be successful. They are mentors who take the time to teach us in areas where we are not yet experienced. The lessons we learn from them can save us from making mistakes both large and small. We should remember that sometimes our role models don't even know we are watching them. In the same way, there are probably others watching us. Knowing that stimulates us to seek the Father's guidance.

There are precautions to remember in looking toward another human being as an example. No matter how much we respect them and how well they have done in the past, we must remember that no person on this earth is perfect. So when that person we have put on a pedestal slips, we must be careful not to be angry or terribly disappointed that they have made a mistake. Jesus is the only perfect example we have to model our lives after. Another caution in having a role model is that we are each created an original by God! He does not create prototypes to copy; so we need to consider our unique personality, circumstances, and relationships, including past experiences and all that makes up our individual life. Then we can make good decisions based on God's Word and the wisdom He offers.

While we have wisely taken time to cultivate our own adult friendships, we have also tried to make a priority of doing things with other families, so the children can be included in conversing with other adults. I think it's important that kids have positive adult role models in addition to their parents.

Many people with small children give up hospitality because of the hassles it entails. I think despite these hassles, it is important (and biblical) for our children to see us open our homes to other people. The key to keeping everyone in our house sane is to set reasonable expectations. If I try to prepare meals from *Bon Appetit* and keep the house in showplace condition, it makes me and subsequently my family uptight. I try to keep things simple and not hide the fact that this is a house where people really live. Reminding myself that few people will refuse to use a less than perfectly clean toilet if they really need to use it helps me keep everything in perspective.

I believe that opening our house to friends and strangers for meals is one way of obeying God's Word. We've had all sizes and shapes of people in our home! Lots of little kids, adopted college kids, missionaries, assorted relatives, church friends, and neighbors have sat around our table. Our children really enjoy having people over. For myself, I thoroughly delight in setting a fancy table (tablecloth, flowers, china, crystal—the whole bit). But I've realized that many people feel the most comfortable when the setting is casual and the food ordinary.

One of the nicest things our friends did for my sons and me after my husband died was to invite us to go with them on their family vacation. It was wonderful for me, as I was worried about how a vacation could be fun without my spouse. We've vacationed with them now for the past seven years, and those memories are so sweet! They've taught my kids to water-ski backwards, plus 360s, slalom, and barefoot. They've also been good role models of a Christian family. I am deeply grateful!

Hospitality doesn't have to be a lot of work or expensive, and it is so rewarding. As young parents, our group of friends got together a lot, and our children came with us (none of us could afford to get sitters very often). The children played together, were bedded down in various rooms, and then were later carried, asleep, to the car for the trip home. A grown daughter of one of our friends, after not seeing us for a long while, heard our voices before she saw us. Later she told her mom that gave her such a warm feeling and brought back so many good memories because it reminded her of when she was little and falling asleep at our get-togethers. I think the children felt secure knowing their parents were together and having a good time. Having an open home is a good environment for our children.

20

Getaways and Time Alone

～⌒⟨Q⟩⌒～

I once heard a family speaker suggest that moms get out of the house completely for one day of the week. It sounds like a good idea, but is sometimes difficult to imagine, much less accomplish, in my house. Many young moms are lucky if they can get away for an hour or two a week, and for single moms it's even harder.

Some people are energized by being with other people; they don't like being alone for too long. I'm the type who's energized by my time alone. I enjoy quiet time to work on projects, read, play the piano, or get a few things done around the house. If I have some respite of peace and quiet each day, I'm better prepared to meet the busy demands of my family. When I miss out on it, I start getting irritable and crabby (just ask my family).

For some, a getaway means a bubble bath and a good book with the door locked. For others, a couple of hours out on a Saturday afternoon helps while hubby or a baby-sitter watches the kids. If you're the type who needs time alone (I can't imagine a mom who doesn't), the point is that it won't just *happen*—we moms need to plan for it. Because we respect ourselves and our need for sanity (as someone has said, "Insanity is heredi-tary—you can get it from your kids"), we're worth the effort.

Ideas from Other Moms

- I have several friends who volunteer along with me at our church youth program each Tuesday evening. We are all young moms, and a few years ago we started going out after the meeting each week for a "ladies night out!" We have had wonderful times sharing pie and coffee or taking in a movie. It's a chance to get away from all the responsibilities and just have fun together.

- My sisters and I live close enough to one another that we plan "sisters weekends" every so often. We get great rates at a hotel with suites, so all of us can stay together. We talk, talk, talk, and laugh, laugh, laugh! Our husbands all agree that it's worth the price of the hotel, because we come back so refreshed; the experience is encouraging and therapeutic.

- After having three children in school, being home alone again with a new baby was a big adjustment. I sometimes found myself restless and feeling cooped up. I was fortunate to have the resources to hire a sitter for the little guy one day a week for about five hours. On that day I accomplished the errands that were extra-hard to take a baby on, and I planned ahead to have lunch or coffee with friends. This really helped me not to feel so isolated.

- For years now my husband has been so great about plan-ning a getaway weekend just for the two of us, usually in January. It may involve hiring a college student or young couple to come and stay with our children, but this is an important thing to do for our marriage *and* family. You see, what we talk about—and keep track of in a notebook—is our family. We discuss each child, one at a time, focusing in on that particular child. We discuss his or her strengths and weaknesses and what action we as parents can take to *help* in his or her needy areas. Is someone shy? We plan to invite friends over more often. Is someone having trouble in reading or math? We plan to buy some workbooks in that area and spend time *together* working on them. If it's an older child, a tutor is considered.

We also look at our marriage. We talk about last year's goals. We look to the future. I remember talking about future summer trips once. Our oldest child was in sixth or seventh grade, and we knew we only had about five or six more summer vacations before that child would leave home for college and would be doing goodness-knows-what in the summers. So we made a dream list of all the places in the U.S. we'd like our children to see—Williamsburg, Washington, D.C., New York City, Yellowstone National Park, Mount Rushmore, the Grand Canyon, etc. We even added England! By the time child #1 graduated from high school, it was great to see how many of these places we'd taken our family to see. And yes, we did get to go to England. What a thrill and privilege to experience the beauty and history of another country with our children!

● Twice a year I go to a hotel alone to renew—to journal, pray, read, sleep, or shop. When I come back, I have a fresher perspective on being a wife and mother.

● For an anniversary gift one year, my husband gave me a certificate for a spa day at an exclusive place in an affluent suburb nearby (Oak Brook, Illinois). I waited to use my certificate, hoping to drop those twenty pounds of extra, unwanted fat that made me look different than those other manicured, shapely, and sharply dressed Oak Brook women. When I hadn't used the certificate five months later, my husband asked if I hadn't liked the gift. Embarrassed, I explained my insecurity and proceeded to make an appointment for my special day. I arrived at 8 A.M. dressed in as classy a way as I knew how and checked in at the desk. Never having been to a spa before, I was feeling a little apprehensive. A lady with a heavy French accent told me to change into a lovely terry robe and lock my clothes and purse in the locker she assigned to me. This was easy, I was thinking—no problem.

As I was getting into my robe, I heard the lady knock at the door of the dressing room. In her heavy accent she said, "Ooooh, you have an Ultimate Spa Day! You'll need to put this on." She handed me an elastic waisted skirt—or so I thought. I put it on under my robe and proceeded to get my next instruction. I was to go to the next room to get a facial. The same lady with the accent asked me to take off my robe so she could give me the facial. Fear struck my bones because I knew that I had only this gathered elastic waisted skirt on and no top! Oh well, we were both women, so I took off the robe! "Oooh," she exclaimed, "you're supposed to have that up around your *neck!*" Embarrassed, I quickly made the change! She was beginning to see the real me—not an Oak Brook woman at all, but an ordinary homemaker.

I told her this was a special gift from my wonderful husband for our anniversary and that I would feel much more relaxed if she would tell me if I made any more faux pas! She then proceeded to give me my facial, but interestingly enough, her accent dropped. She also was trying to be someone she was not! From that moment on, we both had an enjoyable day, both now relaxed and willing to be who we really were. *Lord, help me to be like You, and help me not want to be anything other than the unique individual You created me to be.*

21

Husbands

~~~

When Abraham Lincoln addressed our nation back in 1858, he profoundly said, "A house divided against itself cannot stand." He was referring to our country, but I believe strongly that this is true of marriages as well. Working toward and maintaining a united front when parenting as husband and wife is challenging! God, in His all-wise plan for families, has instructed husbands and wives to love and respect one another. When we stray off the path a bit, that not only affects *our* relationship but also has adverse effects on the credibility quotient we have with our children.

I'm sure we've all observed the security of a child who knows his parents are pulling together on how to guide him, as well as the insecurity of a child who knows his parents can't agree on how to handle him. If parents aren't moving in the same direction on child-raising issues, they are shooting themselves in the feet. If the seeds of a divided front are sown over time, parents will find themselves powerless in the face of their child's or teenager's rebellion.

Here are five practical pieces of wisdom from Sylvia Rimm on how to maintain a united front, taken from her book *How to Parent So Children Will Learn*:

1. Make it clear to your children that you value and respect the intelligence of your spouse. Don't "put the spouse down" except in jest, and only where it's absolutely clear that you're joking. Use conversations with your children to point out the excellent qualities of your husband or wife.

2. Be sure to describe your spouse's career in respectful terms so that you or your spouse aren't feeling as if you're doing work that the other doesn't value.

3. Don't join in an alliance with your child against your spouse in any way that suggests disrespect. Sometimes parents do that subtly, as in, "I agree with you, but I'm not sure I can convince your dad." If you communicate to your child that you value his or her other parent, it will almost always be good for your child, for your spouse, and for you. Be particularly careful during adolescence. Just a few slips may initiate rebellion.

4. Reassure your oppositional children frequently of their parents' mutual support for them. However, be positively firm in not permitting them to manipulate either of you. They'll be quick to see spouse support of each other as a betrayal of themselves and will feel hurt and depressed. Since they're in a habit of seeing relationships between others as betrayals of commitments to them, you should assure them frequently that spouses can respect each other while both still love their children. This is a difficult reality for these youths to cope with, and they may feel emotionally isolated unless they're reassured. One of the parents (the "good" one) will be placed in the position of mediator by these children, in order to persuade the other, unless the parent absolutely refuses to play that role.

5. When your children come to you to complain about their father or mother expecting too much of them, they do that because they're hoping that you'll support their easy-way-out position and that you'll side with them. They're hoping you'll help them "get out of" what the other parent has asked them to do. You want to respond in kindness while maintaining a message of respect for your spouse.[26]

Ideas from Other Moms

I have to give credit to the person who helps balance out my mothering, and that is, of course, my husband! Where I bring a black-and-white perspective to issues, which can polarize things, he brings a spirit of compromise and healing. Where I may be too rigid, he brings flexibility.

Most of us would agree that it's extremely important for the husband-wife relationship to be primary in the family. Still, it's hard to find time to foster that relationship. We've found that planning far ahead and setting up two or three dates a month is well worth it. Although this is time away from our kids, they end up benefiting by the increased intimacy between their parents.

My in-laws have a great family and marriage. With eight children, their weekly date was sometimes their only chance to have an extended private conversation. In my own marriage I can see the difference in our relationship if we're able to spend an evening out alone every week or two. If the budget is tight, then we just go out for coffee and ask another couple to watch the kids, then return the favor.

I believe that setting an example to my daughters about how to treat a husband will speak far more than words ever would. I never allow my children to be disrespectful in any way to their father. So many television programs today portray men and dads as dumb and insensitive. I show the girls that their dad is important in our house and that even though he is a lot of *fun*, they need to show respect for him.

● Taking time out to nurture our marriage relationship is important to me. We carve out time for two getaways each year that will continue to help our marriage grow. It's important to us that we leave the hectic pace of home and kids for several days and devote time to each other. It can be a challenge to find places for the kids to stay or find someone to stay with them. The day before we leave, I find myself asking, "Is this really worth all the effort?" And then when we get away, I reply, "Yes." The dividends are great.

● My husband is my best friend. I love him with all my heart, but I also *like* him. This means that I crave time with him. Even though he travels a lot and we are truly busy with four kids and their activities, we've always made it a point to have some time together. Nothing formulaic, you understand. . . . Maybe we go out for a meal, or for dinner and a show. Sometimes it's just a walk to the park. Other times we take a cup of tea up to the bedroom to talk and lock the door. Whatever it is, we make sure we are alone for a while. When the kids were little, I determined to take time to be alone and not feel guilty about it. It's definitely been worth it.

● When we had young children, we used to trade date nights out with another young family. One Friday night a month they watched our kids all night at their house and we had our house all to ourselves. That was a strange feeling at first! Then another Friday night we traded, and it was their turn to have a night alone. The family with all the kids had a huge slumber party, and the kids loved it. Every now and then we got together as families for potluck dinners.

● Dates with husbands are possible even on a slim budget. There were times when we had only enough money for the baby-sitter and nothing left for our date. But we went out anyway. We picked up a cup of coffee and parked somewhere quiet to talk or went for a walk. When the kids were small enough that riding in the car put them to sleep, we put them in the car in their pajamas, brought munchies, and took a long drive, talking while they slept.

● I'm trying to convey to my children that although I love them, their dad is first with me, after God! Even though the day might be busy with car pools and my part-time job, I try to have the table set and dinner at least started by the time my husband gets home. I also aim to have the house picked up (not including my kids' rooms!) before his arrival. When my husband walks through the door after a long day at the office, he likes a tidy home and the smell of something good on the stove. This takes a lot of organization ahead of time, but it's worth the result.

● One year on our anniversary I surprised my husband by arranging time alone at a hotel. I didn't feel I could leave our children for the night because one was still breastfeeding. So after lunch on Saturday, I picked up our baby-sitter and got the kids settled at home. I kidnapped my husband, took him to a hotel, and we enjoyed a few hours alone. Later that afternoon we went back home and picked up the kids. After taking the sitter home, the whole family went back to the hotel and spent the night together.

22

Keepsakes and Art Projects

"A kiss from my mother made me a painter," said the veteran artist, Benjamin West, after he had won fame and hung his pictures in Royal Academies. When she looked at his first boyish sketch, she praised it; if she had been a silly or sulky parent, she might have said, "Foolish child, don't waste your time on such daubs," and so have quenched the first spark of his ambition.[27]

*I*t's so true that most of what we praise a child for comes to pass! I believe that moms have special opportunities to be prophetic with their children—to notice what they're doing well and give honest compliments, paving the way for more of the same good attitude or behavior in the future. I've seen this happen many times with my piano students. "I loved your crescendo in measure 9!" I'll say. You can bet that each time the student plays the piece, the crescendo will be there, and they'll usually look for other crescendos in other compositions because someone noticed and affirmed them previously. Artwork and keepsakes do that for our children. Each time we hang up their work, display their project as a centerpiece, or show their creation to a relative or friend, they are affirmed. And who knows? One of our kids might become a famous artist someday!

Ideas from Other Moms

Art

● Starting in grade school our children have chosen a few pieces of special art each school year to be displayed. These are framed inexpensively and hung in their bedrooms and the family room. We even send some to grandparents to hang in their homes or a summer cottage. The art is rotating, and different pieces change places frequently.

● We built a treehouse in our backyard that was a wonderful family project. Our children worked with my husband to sketch, plan, measure, and get cost estimates for various-sized treehouses. Then we shopped and watched for sales on the items we needed. The measuring, sawing, hammering, and drilling was hard work. The treehouse we now have is not only a lot of fun to play in, it is the site of many memories of our family working together to accomplish a project.

● When art projects first come home, we display them on the refrigerator or a bulletin board in the kitchen. Later on we hang them on the basement walls. Since kids are the ones who play down there, they get to enjoy their artwork for a long time.

● Coming up with gift ideas for grandparents can be difficult—they always seem to have everything they need. We wanted the children to make something for them that would be meaningful yet practical. Two of our better ideas were these:

Our girls each drew a picture with a black fine-point felt-tip marker that would fit at the top of a half-sheet of paper. We then took the picture to a printer and had them make notepads. They cut a stack of multi-colored sheets in half and attached the sheets at the top so one sheet can be torn off at a time. It was fun for our girls to get notes from their grandparents on their own stationery!

When our children turn four, we have them draw a self-portrait on a sheet of nice quality drawing paper, also printing their name and age at the bottom. For each portrait we purchase similar frames from a do-it-yourself frame shop. The pictures look nice in a grouping on their grandparents' wall.

Keepsakes

● What do we do with all the papers, artwork, and memorabilia from school, church, and friends' homes? Keep an expandable legal-sized pocket folder (1.5–2 inches wide) for each child's school year and label it accordingly. Allow the children to choose what they want to keep most, knowing it must fit in the pocket. If something desired is too large and won't fit, take a picture of it and include the snapshot. This process helps our children to be selective and is highly rewarding; they enjoy going through past years' pockets and reminiscing.

● My son Erik, age four, is a pack rat. I was continually battling to keep his "treasures" organized. Recently I discovered that Rubbermaid sells a "treasure chest" for approximately $10. This has been $10 well spent. All of his treasures are now in one location in an attractive package.

● Each of my children has a drawer in the kitchen. This is kind of difficult in a small kitchen but is worth the effort. We deposit school papers they want to keep, small doodads they come home with, baseball cards, Sunday school papers, etc. Then when they say "Where's that picture I drew last month of Michael Jordan?" or "Where's that prize?" they always know the place I will have put their extras. Every couple of months, when the drawer is exploding, I have them sort through and throw out things that are not as important to them or no longer matter. (I do this myself from time to time!)

- I have a book in which I write down each of the children's birth experiences, cute things they have said, and spiritual milestones. They love to hear about their past.

- I have a large Rubbermaid box (the under-the bed-storage kind that incidentally also fits perfectly under the middle seat of a minivan for food on trips) for each child. Any paper or scrap or award I want to save slips into that box. At fifth grade graduation, I took all of my daughter's artwork and put some of my favorites into a collage in a huge poster-size frame. She had fun admiring all her primary artwork, and it was a nice acknowledgment that she was moving on to a new phase of life. Now that work is preserved, and I plan to do the same with each of the other children. Someday I'll have four masterpieces to display (in the basement?).

- Choose one or two small toys or other keepsake items for each child, and make each into a Christmas tree ornament by tying a string on it or putting it in a little basket.

- Boy, oh boy, do we have a mess on our hands if we don't decide early on (like preschool!) *where* we're going to put the important drawings, papers, and reports our children bring home from school. Obviously we can't keep every-thing! But if there's a designated place for each child, life will have a lot less clutter. We've used Stacks on Steel. These are large black drawers made out of sturdy cardboard, with drawer pulls, and we keep them in our basement. They are manufactured by Fellowes and stack safely on top of each other within a metal framework.

● Years ago I couldn't stand to throw away Christmas pictures that had been sent by friends and family. I started a special Christmas photo album one January in which I put all of the photos before I threw away the cards. We now have over twelve years of great photos that the kids love to pore over.

● With four children under the age of seven, it wasn't possible to spend hours poring over baby scrapbooks; but I am sentimental and knew that someday it would all be important to me. Instead I used a calendar with one week on each page. As milestones were reached, funny things said or done, I wrote it on the calendar in a different color pen for each child. At the end of each year, I went back and filled in their books all at once. The secret to the calendar was that I knew exactly the age at which the events happened and didn't have to guess (was that three months or four months?).

● Collections of my children's music, art, and church awards are kept and displayed in shadowbox frames that have a hinged opening in the back. Bulky items fit in well, and the collection can be changed as new items are received. The framed shadowbox is hung on the wall of each child's room. These boxes can be made or purchased at an art or framing shop.

23

Laundry

teacher had just given her second-grade class a lesson on magnets. Now came the question session, and she asked a little boy, 'My name starts with an *M* and I pick up things. What am I?' The boy replied instantly, 'A mother.'"[28] That certainly seems to be part of a mom's job description!

We moms sometimes get to feeling a bit taken for granted when it comes to the subject of laundry. How it gets collected and how it gets done is different in each family. Some moms I talked to don't mind going around the house picking up, collecting, and doing all the laundry themselves, right down to delivering folded clothes to the proper dresser drawer of each child. Other moms don't do any laundry; someone else in the family (husband or teenager) has that job. Many are somewhere in between. As with other family chores, there's no right and wrong here. It's a matter of what works best in each family. But if a change is necessary, the mom is probably the one to get the ball rolling!

Ideas from Other Moms

- My children, ages two and four, fold the towels and wash-cloths for me. I pay them a penny for each item they fold. They are learning to count, and they are also learning that five pennies equal a nickel and ten pennies equal a dime. We talk about colors and shapes, and they enjoy the chore!

- My husband has installed a series of racks in our laundry area that has made my laundry situation significantly more organized and manageable. Each rack holds a laundry basket. I have one for whites, one for darks, one for brights, and one for special care. Now I sort my laundry into these baskets when my hamper is full, and when the laundry basket is full, I know I have a full load. This prevents laundry piles all over my floor and has significantly cut down on my number of small loads.

- My theory about laundry is that I would rather wash a small load every day than do a huge amount of washing once or twice a week. It doesn't take much time to wash and fold a small amount of clothes. Children need to know how to do laundry too, so they don't have pink underwear in college! Ours began doing their own in later high-school years and were taught how to do so properly. From then on, I only did their clothes if they asked me to during an especially busy time, and then they were much more appreciative! P.S. I don't do shirts! They go to the cleaners!

- Being able to do the laundry is a life skill that everyone needs to learn. An easy way to teach a child is to have them do the sheets each week. The first week, I showed my daughter how to put in the soap and make the correct selections on the washer. After that she developed the habit of washing the sheets from her bed and our bed every Tuesday. Age nine seemed an appropriate age to begin.

I can't exactly afford a plane ticket to Hawaii with the coins and bills that make their way through my washer and dryer, but whenever I find money, I save it until I have enough to take the kids out for ice cream or pie.

In large families, we need methods of knowing which clothes belong to whom. Using a permanent marker, I mark clothing items with a dot system. The oldest child is one dot, the second child two dots, etc. I even mark dots on the bottom of white socks. It really helps when I'm folding a big batch of laundry. As the child outgrows the item, I just add another dot and pass it down!

Laundry is a nightmare around here. I was constantly getting it washed and dried and in baskets, but then it sat in that state until I could sort it all. Now I fold items right out of the dryer on a big table and place each person's clothes in their own basket. The kids can just come down and get their basket when they are low on clothes, put it in drawers, and return the baskets. OK, maybe this will only happen in a perfect world. I admit I end up delivering the clothes, but at least our bedroom is no longer filled with laundry waiting to be sorted.

Any mom doing laundry is somewhat of a chemist. Who would ever guess the thrill of a stain that's removed or the discovery of a product that works wonders? Don't you love a good laundry tip? Here are a few of my favorites:

- Hair spray removes pen marks.
- Peroxide removes blood stains.
- Clorox, Cascade, and boiling water remove baby drool. This is especially useful when putting things away permanently in the cedar chest.

Our family has five baskets in the laundry room, labeled white, light, dark, red, and cold water. Each family member sorts their dirty laundry into one of the baskets. Then, after the clothes are washed and dried, I sort the clothes into five more baskets, one for each member of the family. Then *they* are responsible to fold the clothes and put them away (or to iron the clothes because they *forgot* to put them away!).

● Of course there's laundry—there will *always* be laundry. At first it's a task of mere *importance*—in a new apartment, during the first year of college, or when newly married. Then it becomes a task of *repetition*. It is representative of many tasks in life that can grow wearisome, having to be repeated over . . . and over . . . and over. But—

> As you throw in those loads,
> And close that lid fast,
> Say a quick prayer of blessing,
> For the recipients of this task.

Is it for the husband that left for his daily work? Is it for the child gone for the day to school? Is it for the teenager (the one whose folded shirts were thrown back in the laundry before they were ever worn)? Is it for the guest who just left after a few days' visit? Is it for the neighbor—the one having a crisis and you are there to lend a hand? You have served many through these endless loads; think of whose life you have touched today!

● After a load of laundry is finished drying, fabric softener sheets have one more wonderful purpose—taking the dust off television and computer screens. Their anti-static quality easily removes dust and keeps it off longer.

24

Manners

When I hear the word *manners*, I think first of "Please," "Thank you," "Excuse me," using a napkin at the dinner table, and other forms of polite talk or behavior. All of the above are good habits to teach our children, and if we work on them consistently, by the time our children leave home they just might think to do these things even when we're not around! One concern I have about manners is that they be taught from the inside out, as opposed to being encouraged primarily for outward appearance.

If I am teaching and modeling kindness, patience, loyalty, and honesty to my children, their lives will show evidence of it. Unfortunately, the flip side of this is also true. If I'm not modeling and teaching those qualities, that too will show. The manners I want my life and my children's lives to demonstrate come only through vital contact with and surrender to the Lord Jesus Christ, the One who has unlimited resources of all these qualities and more. These are outlined in one of my favorite hymns, "May the Mind of Christ, My Savior," written by Kate Wilkinson (1859–1928).

May the mind of Christ, my Savior,
Live in me from day to day,
By His love and pow'r controlling
All I do and say.
May the word of God dwell richly
In my heart from hour to hour,
So that all may see I triumph
Only through His pow'r.
May the peace of God my Father
Rule my life in ev'rything,
That I may be calm to comfort
Sick and sorrowing.
May the love of Jesus fill me
As the waters fill the sea;
Him exalting, self abasing—
This is victory.
May I run the race before me,
Strong and brave to face the foe,
Looking only unto Jesus
As I onward go.
May His beauty rest upon me
As I seek the lost to win,
And may they forget the channel,
Seeing only Him.

Ideas from Other Moms

I teach my children to do three things when being introduced
to someone: (1) Smile. (2) Say "Hello." (3) Ask the other person
a question.

This takes the attention off of the kids if they feel awkward,
and a question gets the other person talking—which most
people enjoy doing. This is also good advice for adults!

Polite and well-mannered children are fun to be around. At
two years old, our son already knows and understands the
basics such as "Please," "Thank you," "Excuse me," "I sorry,"

and "Bless you." I believe he has learned these things well because we practice them ourselves. When he says, "Thank you," he is pleasant and sounds like he means it. When he says, "I sorry," a hug usually follows! It is my prayer that Brady will not only be liked by his peers, but also by his teachers and any other adults he comes in contact with.

My ideas on manners are concise: start early, and set a good example. My husband often uses the phrase in our home, "Bad manners are never funny."

I feel that my husband and I had an advantage in beginning our family after almost ten years of marriage. As I watched most of my friends have their babies and begin the process of raising them before I had my own, I could see some things that I would do the same and some that I would do differently. One thing that I didn't agree with was "child-proofing" the house, meaning moving anything and everything that the curious toddler could get into up and out of the way. I have seen homes with nothing below waist level—coffee tables cleaned off and bookshelves void of anything but toys for baby. I feel that the home is where the child first learns to respect property—his own, as well as that of others. Yes, it is more difficult to follow a toddler around, telling him or her "Don't touch" or "If you want to see, let Mommy show it to you." But it's worth the effort when you go into other homes and your little one is welcome because he or she has learned not to pick up and play with every knickknack in sight. I think learning to respect the property of others is foundational in learning respect for others and treating them as we would like to be treated.

If your home is like ours, writing thank-you notes for gifts the children receive is easy to put off. As soon as the kids are old enough to print, we tell them they can't spend it, use it, or wear it until they send a note of thanks. It's amazing how quickly they get the job done!

● I wanted my children to eat properly; so I fed them until they were old enough to hold their utensils correctly. Since their first use of utensils was correct, I never had to break a bad habit in order to teach a good one.

● Manners can be taught to kids before they can even walk or talk. While my children were babies, I started by saying please and thank you (ta-ta). If they coughed, they were taught to cover their mouths. Telephone manners are important in our home; if the children don't exercise good manners, phone privileges are taken away. My children have been instructed not to call any adult by their first name; Mr., Mrs., Miss, Aunt, or Uncle is required.

● We have always tried to emphasize that our home needs to be a safe place, a place where you can be yourself and not be criticized or laughed at. We try to respect each other's property and privacy. At times over the years, when any family member had shortcomings in the above-mentioned areas, he or she has been asked to put a nickel in a can saved for this purpose, or even a dime or a quarter. Ugh! The longer it takes for that money to accumulate, the better I like it. We have shared a number of special treats over the years with the money from the can! Nothing, however, takes the place of a simple apology when needed. Even if it sometimes seems insincere or routine, this is a good habit to establish.

● I have often said to my daughter, "Would you do that if you were having dinner with your future husband's family?" I think our children need to be reminded that bad manners practiced at home may sneak out to embarrass them when they are away from home.

● My kids know the rule: If you ask Mommy something while she's on the phone, the answer is no. This helped my kids learn that unless there was a national emergency, it was smart to wait until Mom was done.

● At one time our children's table manners were quite lacking, so I found a little toy pig and started a pig award. It was passed around the table to whoever was found to be lacking in table manners. The pig then stayed with them until someone else committed an infraction. The person with the pig at the end of the meal cleared the table.

● When our family is out at a restaurant and I need my kids to sit still while the adults visit a little longer, I've been known to pay them each a penny a minute to sit still. It works!

● We have been trying to convince our five-year-old daughter to stop picking her nose. Recently catching her in the act, I said, "Don't do that!"—to which she responded, "I was just putting it back!"

● When Judd was about four, he and I were at an open house and were standing in the food line. A man who had just finished eating walked by, and I noticed that he was even shorter than my 5'3". Judd noticed too and said, not in a quiet voice, "Look, there's a *really* short man!" I got down on Judd's eye level and told him quietly that it was rude to so plainly point that out and that we didn't want to hurt the man's feelings. He responded to my admonition by saying in a *loud* stage whisper, "But, Mom, I just said it because *he is so very short!*" I hope my red face wasn't too evident!

● Our kids are listening all the time, as our middle child showed us when she was about four years old. She came running to tell me that someone was on the phone for me. When I asked who it was, she replied, "Oh, you know, Mom, that not-interesting person!" Puzzled, I picked up the phone and listened to a sales pitch. The light dawned as I heard myself saying, "I'm not interested, thank you!"

25

Moms of Children with Special Needs

~~~

*Y*ears ago my friend and neighbor, Beth, delivered twins. When Sarah and Lauren were born, Sarah, the larger twin, was fine; but Lauren, a bit smaller, did not breathe for two minutes. Lauren stayed in the hospital for three weeks. In the months following, Beth and her husband, Ray, sensed that Lauren's development was slower than Sarah's, and by the time Lauren was eight months old, she was diagnosed as having cerebral palsy. Since that initial diagnosis, Lauren's needs have added regular therapy sessions, leg braces, eye surgeries, seizures, medications, and major leg surgeries to the family's life. Lauren is a delightful young woman with a cute smile, a good sense of humor, and two loving sisters, Sarah and Meredith.

Having lived next door to their family for eight years, I observed that having a child with special needs adds a whole extra dynamic to family life. More than once I sat at my kitchen table with misty eyes, watching the love and care given to Lauren as her sisters played soccer with her in the yard, or as her parents carried her to the car or walked her to her special school bus. I am pleased to include the topic in this book because some of you are moms of a child with special needs, but also for the benefit of moms like me who need more education about how some of our friends deal with children who have special needs. I am drawing on the life experiences of my friends Beth Chase, Nancy Hensley, and Sharon Kettinger for this section, and I'm sure you will find their insights and experiences most honest and helpful.

How Do You Deal with Doctors?

All three moms said that when their children were first diagnosed as having handicaps, they as parents hung on every word their doctors said. But as time passed, that changed. They agreed that gaining all the available information from the doctors is an excellent beginning, but that is only one piece of the puzzle. Sharon did research on doctors, medicine, and surgical procedures having to do with her son's condition. She discovered a Down syndrome clinic that acts as a clearing house for a patient's treatment and now provides a yearly work-up on B.J. Even though the clinic is not local, she said it's definitely worth the trip. Sharon has also kept a medical notebook in which she records everything doctors and medical personnel say at B.J.'s visits, as well as all the medications prescribed. Even though parents are allowed to have reports of all medical details surrounding the birth of their child, they don't always realize the reports are available to them. These reports sometimes become even more significant and helpful as time goes on.

Beth suggested that networking with other parents has been helpful in locating good doctors for Lauren. As Beth interfaces with other moms of children with cerebral palsy through school and Easter Seals, names of the better doctors surface in conversations. According to Beth, continuity with doctors can be quite challenging. Lauren, fifteen, is dealing with her fourth neurologist. That's another reason for keeping good records. But the ideal is to find a doctor who plans on being around for a while.

Some doctors treat disabilities with more respect than others. It's important to find doctors who talk to the child with kindness and respect. Beth and her husband have told Lauren that now that she's a teenager, if there's a doctor she doesn't feel comfortable with, they are willing to look for a new one. Nancy, whose son Christopher has Down syndrome, proposed that interviewing a doctor can be helpful. Not only are parents interested in the medical background and expertise of the doctor, but just as much in how he or she relates with both the parents and the child.

All three moms have had some helpful doctors, but they've also experienced times when they received some comments cautiously. One hurtful comment from a doctor to Sharon was spoken when her son with Down syndrome was an infant: "This baby will never have an IQ of over 25 or 30, but he's going to give you a lot of love." That comment would have been better left unsaid. It's important to weigh all the comments and suggestions from the medical community with some degree of caution, because they are not the ones living with the child. All three moms suggest becoming as much of a mini-expert as a mom can, incorporating all the helpful ideas and information possible, realizing that not everything medical personnel suggest will work in every situation. Medical knowledge is changing so rapidly that the pediatricians cannot be expected to know all the latest research in every area of medicine. Parents need to read, read, read!

What Are the Challenges to Siblings of a Disabled Child?

Sadness, anger, guilt, embarrassment: siblings of a handicapped child experience almost all the same feelings their parents do. And like them, they encounter these feelings over and over again each time a new hurdle arises. In the same way that parents sometimes wish for a non-handicapped child, siblings sometimes wish for a "real" brother or sister, one with whom they could better share their time and feelings. And one who wouldn't make so many problems for them.[29]

Some children feel guilty that they are normal when the handicapped sibling is not. These feelings need to be worked through and discussed as much as is necessary. The key word here is: talk, talk, talk! Nancy suggested that it's important to let the non-handicapped child be his or her own person. Affirm the siblings; give them time and attention. Frequently they don't get as much attention from outside people as the child with the disability.

All three moms agreed that a sense of responsibility for the child with a disability can be a heavy load for a sibling to carry. Parents want to encourage helpfulness and respect without expecting the child to be a mini-parent. It's a challenge to find the right balance. When a mom notices a sibling being unusually angry or impatient with the child who has a handicap, it's time to get the sibling talking about his or her feelings, because there's probably something going on beneath the surface that needs to be dealt with.

Beth advised that a younger sibling be encouraged not to take advantage of or play tricks on the child with the handicap, in spite of the fact that the younger one can outdo the other. Sharon said that even in a situation where a sibling is many years older than the child with a handicap, difficulties can surface. The older child is often ignored in cases like these, while the special needs child is showered with attention. Life can slow down and be challenging for an older child in this position.

In spite of the fact that there are challenges to siblings of children with handicaps, I read a positive statement about this group of people:

> . . . studies show that siblings of handicapped children tend to have a *greater* tolerance for human differences, and a *greater* sense of family bonds than other people. Linda describes her son's relationship with his brothers and sisters: "Around the house Steven has to fight like all the rest. They don't give him any special privileges or let him get away with anything. But when they're playing outside, if another kid picks on Steven or makes a wisecrack, they're all over him. No one else can do that to their brother!"[30]

How Do You Work with School Professionals?

Very carefully, according to Beth, Nancy, and Sharon. As I listened to these moms talk about the process of working with educators, I realized that there's a tremendous challenge in finding a healthy balance between physical needs/therapy and maximizing learning potential/academic thrust. For example, when a child with cerebral palsy goes to Easter Seals for therapy, the therapist works on a long-range continuum for the child's progress, which is medically based. When the child goes to school, the question the school asks is, "What's the best use of our time with this child while he's here?" Their approach is to maximize learning potential and develop an academic program. The tricky part is deciding how that's going to be implemented. In the end, the parent has to take what the doctor says, what the therapists at Easter Seals say, and what the educators say, and be diplomatic in communicating and coordinating all of that information; the parent needs to be the monitor. If school personnel act as though they know all the answers, the parent may come away feeling intimidated, even though nobody knows the child like the parent. The situations that are most successful, according to these moms, are settings where the professional educators see the parents as part of a team in which they all work together with mutual respect for the child's benefit.

Some of the suggestions these moms made were:

- Make sure that school therapy is coordinated with outside therapy.
- Keep a notebook of *everything*.
- Make sure your child gets *outside* therapy; school should not be the only place (this depends on the severity of the need).
- Request a team approach.
- Pray for advocates for your special needs child—someone in the field who will help observe and encourage. Beth shared how much she appreciated a speech therapist who made a special trip, unannounced, to Lauren's school and stood outside the classroom door with tears in her eyes because she was so pleased with Lauren's progress. Advocates like this pave the way for more success.
- Be diplomatic, and learn the art of healthy communication.
- Seek out private speech therapy if your child needs it.
- Stay in touch with the principal because the principal frequently sets the tone and attitude for special needs programs within the school.

There are many educational opportunities available to the special needs child, but in order to get the best possible program, parents need to be actively involved. They cannot afford to depend only on the school.

Much of the responsibility for your child's education falls on you. It's up to you to coordinate and monitor the many elements that have to work together for your child to get the services he needs. It's a time-consuming task, and some parents find it helpful to think of it as their "job." Barb Buswell: "Thinking of myself as Wilson's 'case manager' makes it easier for me to ask for the things he needs. When I think I can't ask for something *else* for Wilson because they'll think, 'She's a pushy mother,' I remember, 'I'm the manager; it's my job to ask.' Sometimes I feel overwhelmed. How can I evaluate this program? How do I know this is best? Then I remember that it's a team approach. I'm not in it alone. It's just my job to get the specialists I trust to talk to each other about it. I remind myself that they know programs, and I know Wilson."[31]

How Have Friends and Relatives Been Helpful? Hurtful?

Nancy greatly appreciates having a sister-in-law who works in special education. She's been supportive emotionally and helpful with information, and Nancy believes that this has been one of God's provisions for helping her along. Beth has a friend, Sandy, who also has a child with a severe handicap. When Beth's daughter was diagnosed as having cerebral palsy, Sandy gave her a big hug and said, "Beth, it's probably going to take at least two years to come to grips with all of this." Beth said that although the words may not have been what she *wanted* to hear, they were loving, honest, and realistic, and Beth remembered them many times. They were words that helped her give herself space in the days to come. Sharon is thankful for B.J.'s grandparents who have visited him at school and have visited support groups and therapy sessions with the family. Nancy fondly remembers a friend who stopped by shortly after Christopher's birth and asked if she could take Nancy's daughter, Kate, out for something to eat. That act of kindness meant a lot to the family.

All three moms appreciate their friends who have stuck by them over the long term. Unfortunately, there are many who fall away, and the social circle of parents having a child with a handicap tends to narrow drastically. Nancy recounted how touched she was by a visit from her sister-in-law, who had recently birthed a stillborn baby. When her sister-in-law visited Nancy and held Christopher, who had just been born with Down syndrome, she whispered to Nancy, "I've never held a *live* baby before."

I chose to include accounts of things that have been hurtful to families with a handicapped child because I have been personally enlightened by these moms, as I believe you, the reader, will be. It is hurtful to parents of a child with a handicap when friends or family don't want to accept the idea that the child may not be able to do things like read, walk, or run. All three moms said that people need to be patiently educated by the parents and to remember that some cases are more challenging than others. It can be helpful for these family members or friends to go along with the family to support group meetings, which can also be educational. Another challenge posed by family and friends is high expectations that put a heavy burden on the mom, insinuating that "If you'd just work harder with the child, he or she would do better." This approach is interpreted by moms as lacking in understanding and empathy.

One mom had a friend who inferred about the birth of her son with Down syndrome, "Didn't you know ahead of time? Why did you birth this child?" That kind of friendship is not a keeper; what's needed are friends who are supportive. In some cases, parents feel that their family or friends fail to see them beyond the needs of the child; the child "defines" the parent. People who say things to the parent of a child with a handicap such as, "God only gives special kids to special parents" or "God has a purpose in this" probably mean well, but comments like that sound trite and non-empathetic.

Regardless of what your relationship is with relatives and friends, you need not allow yourself or your child to be treated in any way that is uncomfortable for you. If you feel your child is unreasonably spoiled or pampered by someone, you can discourage such treatment. If you feel someone pays particular attention to your handicapped child to the exclusion of your other children, you can let them know that disturbs you. If a certain person depresses you, you can openly discuss your feelings with him or avoid talking to him. You can control the balance and atmosphere in your home and your life by being honest with people.[32]

How Do You See That Your Needs as a Mom Are Met?

- Value yourself. In addition to caring for your family including a child with a special need, be sure to pursue an interest of your own as well.
- Ask your husband to take the child to therapy once a week. That way you get some respite, and time demands are shared a little more evenly.
- If a mom is going to survive, she needs her husband to give her some relief and release time—an afternoon to go shopping or a morning to have breakfast with a friend.
- Don't define yourself in terms of your child's handicap.
- Once in a while, enjoy watching your favorite TV program (this particular mom mentioned watching the Chicago Bulls), even if it means that your disabled child's homework doesn't *all* get done.
- Be realistic about the expectations of medical and educational people. Remember that you're a family first, and sometimes you have to let go of what others suggest or demand in order to put the needs of yourself or another family member first.

What Are Some of the Challenges to Husbands and Wives When There's a Child with a Handicap?

Marital stress is so normal and universal in families with a handicapped child that you shouldn't feel defeated or even surprised at experiencing it. Nor should you feel that you have to handle it by yourselves. The best thing you can do may be to seek help from a marriage counselor. A counselor is frequently able to help parents come to terms with their feelings and help them achieve the open communication they need to be emotional *partners* instead of antagonists. So don't be embarrassed to ask for help. It's a sign of strength to do so.[33]

The women I spoke with agreed that admitting a need is difficult, but that seeking help is extremely beneficial. Because spouses react so differently, a professional counselor can assist in first of all getting issues out on the table, and secondly in working together with the couple to understand and reconcile the differences.

All three women spoke of the need for the husband to *be around*. Sometimes it's easier for the husband to go off and do his own thing, leaving the mother feeling stranded. The responsibility of care for the disabled child needs to be shared between husband and wife in an equitable arrangement. Beth said that when her husband started taking Lauren to her weekly therapy session, it was a big help and encouragement—in terms of scheduling, but also in terms of the relationship. Sharon is grateful that when she and her husband have needed extra help, their friends Jack and Karen have come alongside with encouragement, understanding, and baby-sitting. It's not easy to ask for help because that means admitting a need, but that's a highly healthy way to live. Though the challenges for these moms are many, they spoke of the benefit of learning lessons of unconditional acceptance, being totally dependent on God, and seeing the value of life's simple pleasures. The reality here is that in God's eyes, we are *all* special needs children.

I hope these ideas have been helpful to moms who have children with special needs, but maybe even more helpful to those of us who are their friends. May our actions be loving and our words be gracious, lightening the loads of our friends instead of making them seem heavier to bear.

26

Moms Who Adopt

Enriching and *fascinating* are words that best describe my hours spent with Kathy, Jeanne, Joyce, Karen, and Jennifer, five women who with their husbands chose adoption. Their stories were moving, including laughter and tears; but most of all I came away with a deep sense of respect for each of them. The first attribute they had in common was their strong desire to nurture and love a child. These women wanted children very much. Some chose to adopt because of their own medical conditions and some because they saw great needs around them. Most were unable to conceive after several years. The pain of infertility is a silent, private pain that goes unnoticed by many. Some of these ladies participated in many baby showers for friends and sat through Mother's Day services at church without most people around them having any awareness of the unmet longings deep within their hearts.

For Jeanne, infertility procedures were not possible because of a preexisting medical condition. She thought about adoption, but her husband wasn't wild about the idea . . . until he went on a men's retreat and heard a speaker relate his own adoption story. Arriving home from the retreat, he shared his enthusiasm with Jeanne. She cried, realizing that his heart had mellowed. They decided to proceed and went the route of international adoptions, adopting thirteen-month-old twin boys from Romania. She'll never forget the way God moved in her husband's heart and then provided *two* children!

I found myself admiring the tenacity, vulnerability, and patience of these ladies amidst lots of inquiry and paperwork. For Kathy, adopting began with a phone call to Sunny Ridge Family Center. The process continued with an initial screening and preliminary applications. When Kathy and her husband were accepted as adoptive parents, there were several meetings at which agency and adoption policies were explained; a home study was begun. Kathy said this was time-consuming and hard work but definitely enlightening and rewarding. Lots of papers were filled out, but once all the paperwork was turned in and the home study was complete, the social worker stated, "Consider yourself pregnant."

Adoptive moms I spoke with reacted to this stage differently. Some started preparing immediately. Others waited, thinking, "What if something goes wrong?" Kathy and her husband chose to prepare the nursery and were glad they did. Three weeks before their daughter was born, they welcomed *the* phone call saying they had been chosen by the birth parents. Within a few days they had a meeting at the agency with the birth parents and grandparents. This meeting was reassuring for all involved. The presence of Kathy and her husband inspired confidence in the birth parents that the baby would have a bright future, and the presence of the birth parents provided a past for the child being adopted.

The baby was born on a Wednesday. On Thursday Kathy received a phone call from the social worker relating that the birth mother was having second thoughts—she might keep the baby. That was extremely difficult news for Kathy to hear. Thankfully, things were back on the original track by Friday, and on Saturday Kathy and her husband brought home a beautiful baby girl. The families saw each other again the day of the adoption. The good-bye of the birth parents was extremely emotional. Kathy was deeply moved by the complexity of the choice they'd made. Theirs was an open adoption. They had and continue to have contact (through the agency) with the birth family. The level of openness families choose is up to all the parties involved. Last names and addresses are kept confidential by the agency.

Each adoptive mom I spoke with experienced a unique kind of waiting. Joyce and her husband spent several years on fertility treatments before they decided to begin adoption procedures. Three months after their home study was complete, they still hadn't heard anything. Joyce had taken the last final for her doctoral study and was driving home from the university with a friend when she cried out in frustration. Nothing seemed to be happening. What she didn't know was that the baby she and her husband were about to adopt had been born *that morning.* Within several days Joyce and her husband were notified that they had been chosen as the parents and were to meet their new son the next day!

> It is human to want . . . our lives to proceed along the course we have defined as the way it is "supposed to be." . . . No one chooses infertility, though some may prefer adoption over childbearing. No one wishes for birth parents who are not in a position to competently and lovingly raise them. For some members of the circle, the necessity of adoption may signify a loss of innocence; this may be their first confrontation with life circumstances that are not the way they are "supposed to be."[34]

Reading these words, I was reminded of the truth in Romans 8:25–28:

> If we must keep trusting God for something that hasn't happened yet, it teaches us to wait patiently and confidently. And in the same way—by our faith—the Holy Spirit helps us with our daily problems and in our praying. For we don't even know what we should pray for, nor how to pray as we should;

but the Holy Spirit prays for us with such feeling that it cannot be expressed in words. And the Father who knows all hearts knows, of course, what the Spirit is saying as he pleads for us in harmony with God's own will. And we know that all that happens to us is working for our good if we love God and are fitting into his plans.

I sensed an attractive fragrance coming from the hearts of the women I interviewed. It was the maturity of people who have met with experience in life that was less than perfect, but with God's help they chose to become better, not bitter.

After a complicated first attempt to adopt through an agency, Karen and her husband decided to pursue an international adoption. Due to political complications in Paraguay, their country of choice, nothing was happening on the adoption. In the meantime, they received a phone call from a family at their church who was related to a birth mother looking for adoptive parents. They all met and immediately bonded; Karen and her husband were chosen as adoptive parents. When her new child was only three months old, Karen found out that a baby from Paraguay was also ready to be adopted! After a trip down to South America, they had to come back to the U.S. without the baby and wait two months for everything to become legal.

This wait was one of the most painful times in Karen's life. She broke down as she related the experiences to me. Knowing that Mark would be hers but they would be apart for two months seemed more than she could bear. When the two months were up, Karen's husband went to Paraguay and brought Mark home. At this point Mark was almost one, and his recently adopted brother was five months old. The interesting sequel to these two adoptions is that when her boys were both three years old, Karen became pregnant and had twins! They are presently a *very* busy family!

Until I interviewed adoptive moms, I had no idea of the financial expense involved in adoptions. I was truly amazed. During the six months that Joyce pursued fertility treatments, perganol (a fertility drug) cost $500 a month. Karen and her husband remortgaged their house and borrowed money to finance their Paraguay adoption. Kathy estimated her expenses for a private adoption to be somewhere around $12,000, including agency fees, the adoption, and hospital bills incurred by the birth mother. Adopting twins from Romania, Jeanne and her husband realized more than $25,000 in expenses.

As I sat in Kathy's living room the Sunday afternoon I met with these ladies, I was encouraged by the common denominator of God's provisions to each mom and family. Jennifer had experienced cervical cancer early on in her marriage, and after things settled down, she knew she wanted children. After two and a half to three years of infertility and lots of ups and downs, she and her husband decided to channel some of their love for children into work at an orphanage in Bolivia. This experience only furthered their desire to be parents. When they returned to the States, they began working with an adoption agency. After a year passed, Jennifer had a dream one spring night that she was adopting a baby girl and the agency was asking her to name her daughter. After this dream Jennifer pursued more fertility treatments. The next fall John also had a dream. In his dream it was Christmastime, and he was playfully throwing his little girl up in the air. Without mentioning his dream to Jennifer, John suggested that they immediately finish their adoption papers. She wasn't sure why John was so insistent, but they completed the task.

Jennifer remembers that on December 1 she felt discouraged that she was thirty and still without a child (she would turn thirty-one on December 5). The very next day she got a phone call at work from the adoption agency, announcing that their daughter had been born! Three days before her birthday, Jennifer knew she would soon be a mom. Listening to each of these ladies' stories, I was reminded that just as God has seen and provided through the ages, He still sees and provides for us today.

Every adoption story is unique. Why the birth family is placing a child for adoption (not all birth moms are sixteen and single) and why the adoptive family is seeking to adopt a child all come together as God miraculously creates a family.

I asked these five moms and a few others to share some of their thoughts and ideas on adoption. I hope the information will be encouraging not only to women considering adoption, but also to others like me who had not previously understood the complexity of the process.

Ideas from Other Moms

I believe God works through adoption to bring us just the child He created for us. Adoption is something we have all been through (adopted by God as one of His children), and there are many parallels to be drawn from that. When we are adopted as Christians, we have new "families," we are loved unconditionally by our Father, there is no difference between siblings, etc. All these things are true about adoption on earth too!

We reassure our children that adoption is one of the ways God gives children to mommies and daddies. We talk about people in the Bible who were raised apart from their birth families, like Samuel and Daniel. Joseph and Ruth also lived away from their birth families. Joseph in the New Testament was Jesus' adoptive father. We always talk about our children's birth families in a positive light.

My dad sat down with me three or so years before we adopted and told me that having four little girls was the highlight of his twenties and thirties. He knew we would have a child and was excited about it happening any way possible (including adoption). This set the stage for a great, accepting experience on the part of our families. My mom, on one of the many baby gifts she gave Mary Elizabeth, said, "From the cabbage patch straight into our hearts!"

● Being a part of an adoption support group has been most helpful. We share the common experience of adoption, and we are committed to getting together, rotating the responsibility for monthly meetings.

● Having had two children naturally and then adopting two, I have been reminded that *all* our children are gifts from God. We do not own them. Each child is unique, and we as parents do the best we can to oversee their growth. When our natural children were fifteen and nine, we requested to adopt infants so the older children would be a good distance apart from the younger two. The creative teenager liked playing with the two little ones, and the organized pre-adolescent enjoyed helping with their care.

● I find it awkward when people say to me, "Your daughter is so lucky to be a part of such a good family." First of all, I don't believe in luck. Second of all, she would have been a great daughter to anyone. *We* are the privileged ones to have the opportunity to raise her!

● The laws and attitudes of this country are slowly being altered to protect adoptive families. Follow the rules, be patient, and don't take *any* legal shortcuts.

● We adopted three of our children when they were old enough to understand the significance of the event. To help make the occasion memorable, we had an adoption celebration for each one. We had pizza, a special adoption cake, and lots of balloons. A special Cabbage Patch Kid (adopted with the same name as the child) was a gift to help him or her remember the happy day. As we've had these adoption celebrations, the older adopted children love to look at the photographs of their own celebrations and talk about their special day.

27

Music Lessons

The Piano Teacher
  by Chad Elwell

Faithfully I sat in the old rocker adjacent to the bench;
Waiting patiently for the weekly visits.
Daily they arrived, one after another,
Ready to demonstrate,
To show all that they had prepared.
They looked forward to their time,
Knowing they would see a smile on my face
Every time they entered.
Never too hasty to begin,
I would be sure to listen
As they talked excitedly about all that was important,
And all the things that seem trivial now.
Eventually, they would be ready to start,
And would set in on one piece at a time;
As they played, I listened quietly,
Gently correcting at times:
"Curl your fingers a bit more. Yes, that's it."
"Ah-ah; look at the music, not your hands."
As they played, their practice time became apparent;

None could fool me into believing they had practiced;
Only by performing could I be convinced.
After they completed the material,
I would suggest new things:
"Do this next time."
"Try playing it like this."
And slowly change would come;
Not in one week,
Or a month or season,
But I could tell their progress
And see how far they came,
Always coaxing them,
Encouraging them to be even better musicians,
Pushing them to their limits, and not beyond.
Until it would come time for the session to end.
After the hands of the clock
Had completed their trek around the circle,
They would reluctantly rise.
And they would leave with new studies to perfect,
And the anticipation of next week.

Regarding moms, kids, and music lessons, I, Ellen, write from my experience as a piano teacher and many years of watching my own kids study music. Music is definitely a passion in my life! I'm grateful that God has blessed me with the ability to enjoy and make music.

Ever since I was a young child, I have been inspired and moved by music. Some musicians in the church I grew up in noticed my interest and abilities and encouraged my parents to start me on the violin. They did, when I was nine, and it proved to be the start of a wonderful adventure that I'm still enjoying today. When I was thirteen, some friends who were moving gave my parents a piano. I had always wanted to study, and I still remember the excitement I felt the day the piano was delivered to our house. Beginning piano lessons immediately, I was instantly attached to the instrument. I'm grateful that my parents found me good teachers because I ended up being a piano major in college, and my teaching style and habits now are a compilation of the styles and habits of all the teachers I've ever had.

I frequently receive phone calls from parents asking for advice on music lessons, so I am including some of the questions I hear most often, along with my answers and opinions on each one.

What Type of Music Instruction Is Best?

Many parents wonder, should I enroll my son or daughter in group programs like Kindermusik or Suzuki when they are very young (two to five), wait until grade school music programs begin in fourth and fifth grades, or begin with traditional private lessons? I've done all three. I enrolled our oldest son in Suzuki violin when he was four years old. He studied with one of the top Suzuki teachers in the nation, and she was tremendous. But that only lasted for one and a half years because Chad couldn't have cared less about the violin. I realized after a while that I was doing it more because of my interest in violin, and that wasn't going to keep him going long-term. Other students who enrolled in that same Suzuki class have gone on to be first-class artists, some majoring in music and wanting to be teachers themselves.

The key to Suzuki, I feel, is that parent and child need to be equally dedicated to studying the instrument. The program demands a large investment of time for the parent, and when parent and child work well together, this offers great bonding time as a result. *Suzuki* programs offer group instruction on individual instruments, whereas *Kindermusik* offers group instruction on music and movement in general, sometimes including work at the keyboard. This program provides a great introduction to music for the child who is

186

considering something more down the road. Kindermusik Beginnings is for children eighteen months to three and a half years old and provides a wonderful bonding experience as the child and caregiver explore music and the joy of movement together.

School music programs in our area provide marvelous learning experiences on musical instruments. Our two older boys began studying French horn and oboe when they were in fifth grade, and their schools have offered excellent instruction. We gave them lots of direction in their selection of an instrument. Since Jim and I are both musicians and have played in orchestras, we preferred to have our children studying instruments that could be played in a band or orchestra. We also suggested instruments that not everybody else plays —French horn, oboe, bassoon, viola, or cello, for example. There's always a spot for these instruments when played well. Aside from the benefits of artistic enrichment and music education, we also felt that music groups would provide a social outlet. The camaraderie our boys have experienced in band and orchestra has been great. Our oldest son was drum major of his high school marching band for two years, developing extra skills in leadership and social interaction.

If a child begins studying an instrument in group lessons at school and continues to show interest and ability, parents should look for a good private teacher to help the student gain musical expertise on his instrument. Kids who don't take private lessons tend to pick up some sloppy habits and generally don't progress as well as those who do. All three of our sons studied their instruments privately with excellent teachers—Chad on French horn, Nate on oboe, and Jordan on piano. In addition to the ensemble and group lessons they received at school, their private lessons were invaluable. Besides the expertise their teachers offered on the instruments, each developed a pleasant and enjoyable relationship with his teacher. It's a neat experience for a student to receive a half-hour or hour of undivided attention in their lessons each week.

What's a Good Age to Begin?

If you're considering Kindermusik or Suzuki, children can begin as early as age one and a half. If you're going the route of traditional private piano lessons, I recommend age seven for a girl and eight for a boy. At that point, their small motor skills have usually developed enough to keep up with the signals their brain can send. Kids who start at five or six make slower progress and usually require constant supervision and help from a parent. By the time children are seven or eight, if the parent is willing to sit at the piano with the student the first day or two after a lesson, the child can usually practice on his own for the rest of the week and gradually progress in independence.

What Are the Benefits of Studying Music?
(Ideas from My Friend Ruthie Schroeder)

Studying music:

- Develops positive self-esteem.
- Develops small muscle coordination.
- Develops an interest and skill that can bring children much enjoyment for the rest of their lives.
- Teaches self-discipline and imposed discipline, both of which are essential to success.
- In Suzuki and Kindermusik programs, parent and child have a bonding opportunity as they pursue music together.
- In group programs, a child has opportunities to develop relationships with other children who have a musical interest.

How Should I Select a Teacher?

Before making any phone calls, parents need to decide what kind of teacher they want. Is it a master teacher—someone who is top-notch in his or her field, one who routinely has students winning competitions and being accepted as music majors in colleges around the nation? Is it a teacher with high expectations, one who has a reputation for teaching good music skills to kids who aren't necessarily interested in music as a career but want to learn solid technique and good music with some opportunities for performing? Or is it a desire for a casual, low-key approach teacher who enjoys music as a hobby? There are all of the above in the teaching field.

Once you've decided what you want for your child, start calling friends, church music ministers, local colleges, and music stores to get names and recommendations. You might also call your local chapter of Music Teachers National Association, an organization with quality teachers in every area of music. Once you have a list of names to work from, think about what you want to ask the teacher.

- What is the calendar year?
- What is the length of lessons?
- Are there any group lessons, classes, or performance opportunities?
- What are the expectations of the teacher?
- Do you have a policy sheet you can send in the mail?
- What are your fees for lessons? Do you charge by the lesson . . . monthly . . . quarterly?
- What's your policy on missed lessons?
- Who purchases the music—the teacher or the parent?

When selecting a music teacher for your child, look for a combination of pleasant personality, excellent training, solid experience, and dedication. I might add here that what I lacked in experience when I was fresh out of college, I think

I made up for in enthusiasm! In locating teachers for our children, my husband and I have looked for excellent musicians, but we've also sought teachers who are good role models, have reasonable expectations, and show patience in working with kids.

How Do I Get My Child to Practice Consistently?

The most important factor here is *expectation*. If the teacher and parents don't expect consistent practice, they aren't going to get it!

The second factor is *incentive*. Incentives vary from student to student and studio to studio. I was motivated to practice because of sheer love for the instruments. Some kids need practice charts from the teacher or parent, or little prizes to keep them working. Some need to be kindly reminded, and that's all it takes. One of my friends tells her daughter that when she practices before school in the morning, she gets to stay up a half-hour later at night for reading time. What a great incentive!

The third factor is *accountability*. If practice isn't happening, don't ignore the problem. At one point when my husband and I were spending about twenty-five dollars a week on one son's lessons, we expected him to practice at least five days a week. Since he was in high school at the time, he had *some* money. If he had periods of time when we didn't hear many golden tones coming from his horn, we explained that if he didn't start practicing, he'd have to pay *us* for the days he didn't practice. (At five dollars a day, all he needed to do was *hear* the idea and he got practicing!) Some teachers have practice charts or contracts they hand out regularly or occasionally which can also be helpful tools.

What Are My Responsibilities as a Mom When My Child Is Studying a Musical Instrument?

Oversee practice, and reinforce the teacher's instructions. This may involve listening to the student's practice sessions, talking about the practice plan together, or looking over their lesson assignment, if they have one in writing.

Offer encouragement. Sure, we're going to hear some "clinkers" every now and then, but when we hear the good sounds, we should be calling out, "Great job! You're producing some fine tones!" or "I like your even tempo!"

Keep the instrument in good working condition. Pianos should be tuned once a year, wind instruments need new reeds, brass might need valve oil, and string instruments need rosin, new strings, and bows re-haired.

Communicate with the teacher from time to time. Let him or her know when there's progress and when there are difficulties.

How Do We Know When to Discontinue Lessons?

This is a tough question, and there aren't any absolute answers here, but again I'll respond out of my own experience and thinking. I am convinced that wherever there's a possibility to study a musical instrument, as many children as possible should be given the opportunity. But I don't believe that *every* child who starts should necessarily continue. Because of all the opportunities available to help children develop *their* particular interests and gifts, I believe that the long-term study of music should be reserved for those who truly *like* it! That doesn't mean there aren't going to be some days students don't want to practice or months of dwindled interest. Sometimes interest can be revived with new music or even a change of teachers.

A change of teachers at some points provides a new approach and fresh motivation. But if a child truly *hates* studying an instrument, my opinion is, "Let him switch, take a break, or quit, because music lessons are not for everyone!"

If there's a pattern in all this, it's that a student begins with great enthusiasm. He or she finds the first year or two reasonably easy, and there aren't too many battles at home about practicing. Sometime during the second or third year, things get a little more challenging, and the student may face more of an uphill climb. I have few students stop here. Junior high is the time students experience what I call "the fork in the road." If they don't have many interests other than music, it's good to keep them going on their lessons if they are doing reasonably well and deriving some satisfaction out of the whole experience. However, if music study becomes a battle between student and parents, and the student has other activities he or she is enjoying a lot more, I say let him or her move on to something else.

From my perspective as a teacher, I don't want to teach a student who doesn't want to learn. If a student is interested, continues to make progress, and takes personal responsibility, I'll continue to teach him or her. But I always have a waiting list, and if I sense that a student has been lagging in interest and commitment for a length of time, even after attempts to regroup and refocus, I'll be the one to discontinue lessons. If and when a decision is made to end music lessons and move on to other interests, it's helpful for the parent to call attention to the progress the child realized while studying a particular instrument. Emphasize the positive experience, as opposed to speaking of it in negative terms. It's better to say, "I studied piano for two years" than to say "I quit piano after two years."

28

Organization

~⟨Q⟩~

$\mathcal{I}$s there a mother on the planet who is 100 percent organized? I'd like to meet her! Any mom who's ever had even one child on a sports team knows how hectic life can get! Dinner schedules are interrupted. Chauffering kids across town for all the practices becomes challenging. I chuckled to myself when I overheard another baseball mom describing the scene at her home when one of the stirrups from her son's baseball uniform failed to make it all the way through the laundry cycle. Everyone in the family was running around trying to help him find his stirrup and still make it to the game on time. This slice of family life sounded painfully familiar to me.

I know some moms who are extremely well organized and others who wing it. My sister Gail is probably the most organized person I know. It's delightful to be in her home. Everything has a place, and everything is in its place! There's nothing in her home that she can't locate within a minute or two—even if the desired object is in the attic! She maintains a healthy balance of keeping things orderly while showing worth and value to the people around her.

When I go out walking early in the morning, I often reflect on the order and organization in God's creation. The tulips and daffodils come up at the same time each year. The four seasons come *every* year (although some winters in the Chicago area sure seem like they will last forever!). There's never an autumn when the trees don't shed their leaves. "The heavens are telling the glory of God; they are a marvelous display of his craftsmanship. Day and night they keep on telling about God" (Ps. 19:1-2).

Imagine how we would feel if God mixed up the seasons one year or switched day and night in a twenty-four-hour period. I would feel pretty confused and insecure. There are some changes that we all deal with from time to time, but experiencing God's order is a wonderful thing. In the same way, our children will also face change on occasion, but the more order and organization we can build into their lives, the more secure and confident they will become.

Ideas from Other Moms

The better organized I can be, the more smoothly things seem to go for our family. Having said that, I'm also learning to be flexible. With five young children and a husband who is a busy physician, things often don't go as I plan. At first I feel frustrated, but then I try to move on and accept Plan B. It is important to have plans and be organized even though they may not be carried out, because it becomes frustrating to the whole family if things are forgotten, schedules are missed, things are lost, or everyone is late. Some ideas that help our family are:

- A children's calendar with color codes for each child.
- Lists for groceries.
- Specific baskets for school library books and public library books.

- Out-of-season clothes and hand-me-down clothes in labeled boxes.
- Pairs of mittens put together with clothespins.
- Written schedules for busy days.
- Written goals for each year.

I make lists, lists, and more lists. I have found this to be a wonderful tool, especially when I'm feeling overwhelmed. At least putting it on paper makes me feel as though I have some order and control.

After twelve years in a profession where I was quite goal oriented, being a new mother has often been difficult for me. There are days when I accomplish nothing more than bathing myself and the baby, feeding the baby (and sometimes me), changing diapers, playing on the floor, and preparing dinner. I used to feel discouraged about that until I stopped to think that it took me all day to do these things—that motherhood is a full-time job! The other things I want to do don't often get done. I try not to set too many goals for each day, and that has helped. If I can get one extra thing done while my baby takes his afternoon nap, I feel good. Being flexible has been one of my most valuable assets, because just when I think I have two hours to get something done, he decides he doesn't need to sleep!

When we were preparing to sell our home, I knew I needed some quick ways to get the house in order in case a real estate agent (many of whom now use cellular phones and call from two minutes away) wanted to show the house immediately. I had everything basically clean and ready, but there were always last-minute towels and papers to get rid of and sinks to be cleaned out. We bought laundry baskets and kept them ready in different parts of the house. If someone was coming, the plan was to wipe out the sink with used bath towels (the pretty ones were there to look nice—my family wasn't allowed to use them) and throw them and anything else that was clutter into the basket. Each person had their assigned baskets, and the full baskets were thrown into the trunk of the car. (The car and under the bed are the only places prospective buyers won't look.) Then when we couldn't find something later, we always knew where to look! After the people left, we sorted through the baskets. Fortunately, God knew I would be a crazy person if we had to have a perfectly clean house for too long, and we sold our home the first week!

A good start to church on Sunday can begin as early as Saturday evening. We try to do entertaining and activities on Friday night so that Saturday evening is reserved to get ready for church. Baths begin right after supper. Hair is washed, nails are trimmed, rooms are tidied, and outfits are organized for the next day. Sunday mornings will still be busy, but not as rushed as they would be if we hadn't planned ahead.

For especially busy weeks, I draw up a chart to go along with my calendar and to-do list. I write the days of the week across the top of the paper, and "Morning," "Afternoon," and "Evening" down the side of the paper. The weekend before, I sit down and write in all meetings, appointments, and to-do's in these slots. Everything is then accounted for, and I feel purposeful all day long. I even write in down time that I know I'll need in order to keep going. I also write in exercise times to make sure they happen. At the end of the week I feel good about how I've used my time, and I love to see all that I've crossed off the chart as "done."

Being organized is the only way I can care for my husband, mother my children, manage the house, work a part-time job, and be involved in various church and school activities. My household duties are assigned specific days:

Monday: Laundry and ironing.
Tuesday: Grocery shopping.
Wednesday: Free.
Thursday: Clean house.
Friday: Clean sheets and towels.

Over the years of sticking to this plan, I have been able to keep up with all my household chores. Another big help is a personal calendar that sits near the phone and goes into my purse whenever I go out. Whenever appointments are made, they go right into my little calendar. Grocery items, dry cleaning pickup, fertilizer for the lawn, birthday gifts—all these get recorded too.

I plan at least two major gatherings in my home each year (perhaps kitchen parties or brunches), so I will be motivated to go the extra mile and clean the corners of my house. This also gives my husband a deadline for doing those "little jobs" like hanging a new picture, making small repairs, or fixing up the yard. He usually complains that I am a perfectionist, but he is always glad to see the end results. I rarely am motivated to do a fantastic cleaning for my family, who are never quite as appreciative of my efforts!

Since we all like the satisfaction of crossing tasks off a list when they are completed, to this day my twelve- and thirteen-year-old daughters have checklists on the refrigerator of what they need to accomplish each day—instrument practice, homework, exercise, devotions. They work much better with them than without them.

I insist that family members pick up and put things away before going to bed each night. It's much more pleasant to greet the day in a tidy home.

My friend June visited a friend's house and brought along her two sons. The friend had a son whose bedroom was

197

one of the messiest June had ever seen. "That will teach the boys," she thought. "They'll realize that a super messy room is a disaster, and they'll be motivated to keep their rooms clean." Well, she was right—partially. When they got home, one son reacted the way she had expected, but the other one said, with wide eyes, "Wow, did you see Ken's room? That was so cool—he could have it *exactly* the way he wanted it. And his mom isn't even upset about it. I wish *mine* could be that way!" I guess that just shows how much personalities differ!

My kids do not store money very well, and I seem to find it here and there. We started a system of keeping their money in a family "bank." They each have a blank check register that allows me to put in deposits of allowances, birthday money, etc. They make withdrawals for purchases by subtracting in this book. This serves two purposes: they don't have to have cash with them when we are shopping together but can still make purchases. And this prepares them for balancing a checkbook when they are older.

29

Pets

My Gerbils
by Jordan Elwell, age 9

My gerbils are so cute! Their names are Robinhood and Maid Marian. Their favorite food is sunflower seeds. I like to play with them. They bite and it hurts a little bit. Sometimes I let them loose on the floor, but not while the cat is there! I bought the gerbils at Besser's Pet Shop in downtown Wheaton. The petkeeper said that they will probably have babies. I wonder what they will look like?

I made a trip to Besser's Pet Shop in Wheaton, Illinois, purchasing our fourth water bottle for Jordan's gerbils. The little critters loved to chew right through plastic bottles and the rubber corking on glass bottles. I struggled to find one they couldn't destroy. Was I irritated at the inconvenience? Yes. Am I sorry we were the owners of Robin Hood and Maid Marian? No. They were fun for our whole family. But not all pets work for all families. We discovered that dogs weren't for us after giving it a try and eventually finding the dog a new home. The previous sentence was a nice way for me to say that I am not a dog person, and after two years of the dog "leaking" whenever he got excited, I finally said to my husband and kids, "It's me or the dog."

Since then, cats have been the primary pets for our family. They're cuddly, clean, and easy to take care of. However, many of our friends have dogs that have been marvelous pets for their family. My son Nate recounted a car trip he took with his friend's family and their dog, Max. When the family got off the interstate and stopped at McDonald's for dinner, they ordered hamburgers and fries for everyone—even Max—who quickly snarfed them up. Nate was thoroughly amused!

There may be some trial and error involved in figuring out what works for your family, but pets can be a great source of companionship, providing opportunities for responsibility and lessons in consistency. Beginning with something simple like fish or gerbils and working on up probably isn't a bad idea.

Ideas from Other Moms

● If pets are an option in your family, they can be used to teach many basic principles to children of all ages. Responsibility for care, feeding, walking, and bathing rotates on a weekly basis in our house. Each child is responsible for our dog for one week at a time. We talk often about animal behavior. We also discuss our children's responsibility for their dog's behavior when friends are over, and for the behavior of their friends toward the dog. Basic respect for the care and life of an animal is a good building block for respect and concern toward others.

● My son received two hamsters for Christmas. I have been completely amazed by the hours he and his friends have been entertained by these cute rodents. It has also been a great tool for teaching him responsibility.

● We once had a darling black kitten with white paws—"Sox," we named it. Our youngest child was barely one year old when we were trying to train it to do its duty in the litter box. Unlike most normal cats, Sox refused to use the litter box and did his business in other places. Little did we know that he was leaving it behind a chair in the family room. One afternoon when I was entertaining a lady friend for coffee, I noticed our little girl carefully lining up some small dark objects on the coffee table where we were having our refreshments. You guessed it! She had discovered where Sox was doing his "duty"!

● Before purchasing a pet, decide who's going to do what jobs (walking the dog, feeding the cat). Then write it all down, and have everyone sign their name on the dotted line. This is an early lesson in the meaning of the word *contract*!

● It was a Sunday morning—a rare Sunday morning when the whole family (the author's) was ready for church early. The older boys were dressed, and Jordan (two and a half) looked spiffy in his white turtleneck, plaid pants, and suspenders. I sat down to play the piano for a while. After ten minutes or so, things sounded *too* quiet. Walking through the house, I found Jordan in the laundry room with our white dog. Jordan had gotten into Jim's brown shoe polish and had carefully painted one whole side of the dog. Apparently the dog didn't mind because he was sitting quietly, enjoying the attention. The remarkable thing about this event is that the little guy didn't get one *speck* of shoe polish on himself. It was one of those events that was too cute to get mad about. Instead, I called the rest of the family to come and enjoy the sight!

● Unless you own one, it is tough to understand why people get so committed to a pet. Furry or feathered, soft or scaly, pets add character to a family in such unexpected ways. Personally, I never cared much for dogs, especially when I visited friends and their furry pet gave me a hello lick or sat on my feet during a meal. Ick! Then our children started that well-known process. Every parent has experienced the pleas, the longing eyes, the desperate unsolicited acts of kindness children perform for us, the newspaper "Free Puppy" classifieds circled in bright yellow. Such a deal! And of course the kids made serious promises of uncomplaining care for the chosen pet. We gave in, as hundreds of parents do, and our perfect pet was chosen.

The golden furball of a puppy was picked out of a new litter, and Sandy was ours. Six years later, the seventy-pound, shedding canine has been walked miles and watered gallons and has gone through hundreds of pounds of dog food. Her privileges keep increasing. For instance, she has gone from laundry room sleeping to bedroom sleeping, and from plain dry dog food to dog food supplemented with people food to "make it better." Of course, the "Who wants to walk the dog?" question is met with groans, and usually (as expected) Dad gets the assignment.

Routines are easily established with pets. For us, it is the dog's welcome each morning, her begging for bread when school lunches are being made, the morning walk, and the few quiet moments each evening lounging in the family room for the ten o'clock news. Every day is about the same for Sandy. However, the routine was interrupted unexpectedly when a lump was found during the final pat one evening. It was not a big lump initially, but it grew quickly, and the veterinarian told us it was cancer. What did that mean? Surgery? Therapy? How long? Now what? My mind said, it's just a dog, but my heart said, it's our dog—we have to do what we can.

Surgery went well, and the recovery started. We all talked about the what ifs. Her presence in our family became such a privilege again because her absence for two days left a void. It's funny—when we experience the threat of something being taken away, the value of ownership of that something goes up! Sandy's value to us shot up. The outcome? We're not sure yet. Maybe two years, our veterinarian tells us. We don't complain as much about walking our dog. Each day with her has value to all of us, and she is loved more than ever.

30

Photos

I've heard it said that "nothing is fully appreciated until it is remembered." When I wrote this section, I had just returned home from a Senior Honors Assembly at Wheaton North High School where our son, Chad, received several awards and scholarships. Did I take my camera? You bet! Years down the road, since I'm not so busy *going* to my children's events, I enjoy viewing the photos and appreciating those special moments all over again. We caught the birthday parties, the vacations on the beach, the "first days of school," the Christmas pageants, family holidays, and recitals. Most of them are neatly contained in photo albums, although all my pictures from the last year are still in piles waiting to be organized. Maybe when I'm done compiling and writing this book, I'll get to the photos!

Ideas from Other Moms

● During the month of January—because it's cold outside and there seems to be more spare time during that month—I tackle the project of our photo albums. I put the card table up by the fire and assemble the sometimes hundreds of photos taken during the past year. It usually takes about a week of evenings, and it doesn't look museum-quality, but it gets the job done, and the kids love poring over the pages.

● Several weeks before going to visit out-of-town friends or family, we post photos of the people we will be visiting, frequently pointing them out to our children. Talking about them and seeing pictures helps the younger ones know what to anticipate.

● It is not difficult to keep photos organized if I sit down the day I receive them and spend ten minutes writing down names, events, and dates on the back. I immediately place them in a photo album. Photos that are identical or similar are placed in a separate box to keep for the children. This box is theirs; they use the photos for home or school projects or for making cards or for their own photo albums.

● I treasure all photos of my children, and I want to save them as best I can. I recently attended a photo preservation workshop from a company called Creative Memories. They have local representatives who show how to put together creative albums that not only *protect* our photos but also use a few words and page designs to help save those cherished memories. The supplies are great, and there are monthly work sessions that give fresh ideas.

● During my son's first year, I took a picture of him on each month's anniversary of his birth. When I took the picture, I had the same stuffed animal posed next to him. We were able to see how he had grown each month as we compared his size to the stuffed lamb. I also took a photo on his first birthday and plan to do so on each of his following birthdays. I wonder how he'll cooperate when he's sixteen?

● Photos are memories I want to pass on to my children. I always order double prints when I take film to be developed. When I bring the new pictures home, I sit down and sort through them the same day. Some photos go in our album, and some go in the children's (I'm keeping one for each child). When they leave to go away to college or a career, they will have a pictorial history of life in our family.

● I found it impossible to keep pictures organized until I began purchasing photo boxes from the discount stores. These boxes make it easy to file my photos by events and seasons. They are also less expensive than photo albums and don't require much storage space.

● One of my favorite things to do when visiting my mother is to look at the family photograph albums. They are a great record of our history as a family. Her three children all wish they had their own copies. For that reason, I plan on making an album for each of my children. Each year I will make a two-page spread of the highlights of that year. That way each child can have a piece of my larger family albums for their very own.

● When my daughter was four years old, she was a flower girl in her paternal aunt's wedding in Canada. After receiving the wedding proofs, she was delighted to show them to her maternal grandmother and tell her about each one. As she came to the picture of the bride and groom leaving for their honeymoon, my preschooler exclaimed, "Look, Grandma, here they are going on their field trip!"

31

Prayer

*All that I am or hope to be I owe to my angel
mother. I remember my mother's prayers and
they have always followed me. They have clung
to me all my life. (Abraham Lincoln)*

As I was driving Nate to his high school for baseball
tryouts, I assured him that I would be praying for him. That
comment apparently reminded him of a story he had heard
at his youth group about a mother's prayers for her son. (Nate
loves to tell stories.) Here is the story in a nutshell:

During the Vietnam War, a battalion of soldiers was hover-
ing in a trench while a battle was raging around them. One of
the young soldiers in the trench was aware of a buddy crying
for help, lying wounded out in the open area. The commander
had given orders for everyone to remain in the trenches, but
the restless young soldier kept looking at his watch every few
minutes. All of a sudden he bolted for his wounded buddy,
picked him up, and dashed back to the trench, unharmed.
Later the commander asked the heroic soldier why he had

been looking at his watch so much and why he made the dash. The soldier replied that before he left home, his mom had promised that she would be praying for him at specific times each day, and *that* had been one of them!

By the time Nate finished telling me the story, we were in the front circle drive of his school. At that point I had such a big lump in my throat that all I could do was wave as he got out of the car. Nate smiled and said, "Bye, Mom." It was a special moment. (By the way, he *did* make the baseball team!)

Ideas from Other Moms

● I pray at the sink, in the car, in the doctor's waiting room, with joy, with tears, through hardships, for the future, in all aspects and places of life. Prayer is my lifeline to wisdom, my strength and hope, and my release from stress and fears.

● I have been keeping a prayer journal for about three years now. I usually write in it once or twice a week. The best thing about it has been going back every few months and seeing how God has truly been faithful to our family and is bringing us through tough stuff that has been ongoing. It has given me the hope and will to keep going. I have a record of times when I was crying as I wrote things down, and yet I can see God's answers to my prayers consistently and faithfully over time.

● I like to walk outside, and that's also a good time for me to pray. I've always had trouble praying silently and keeping track of my thoughts. I got a wild idea after watching my girls sunbathing on the beach and singing along with their Walkmans. If I wore headphones when walking and prayed out loud, people would think I was singing along with a tape. Somehow I thought I would look less eccentric that way than if I was just walking around talking to myself. I guess I really do care what people think of me!

During the three and a half years that our son struggled and fought with leukemia, I learned that when things seem out of control, God is still in control of my circumstances. I learned that He gives grace enough to finish each day if I ask Him for endurance. If I believe, He provides. Some of His provisions included:

- A friend who offered to prepare dinner for our family every day that our son had to make a trip to the clinic for treatment.
- Peace of mind.
- Support from a Christian school.
- Friends who volunteered to watch our infant daughter so the rest of us could go to the hospital.
- Family who came to help around the house.
- Kindness from doctors and nurses at the hospital.

After praying with my children each night at bedtime, I encourage them to talk to God about their feelings, fears, and requests. We also pray for others and give thanks. If they don't want to pray, they don't have to, but I suggest that they pray to God silently after I leave the room.

I've tried to make it a practice to tell my children good night as they lie in bed ready for me to turn out their light. And this continues until they leave home for college! What I really want to do is *pray* with them. I try to keep it short because the kids are tired, but it's a wonderful chance to thank God for His goodness and blessings to us that day and to pray about any uncomfortable situation between friends that may have developed or an upcoming test or whatever. I conclude by asking for a good night's rest. Then comes a kiss good night, planted on a forehead or cheek, and I get to remind them, "I love you! Sleep tight! God bless! See you in the morning!"

● Pray, pray, pray . . . No matter what their age, pray with and for your kids. Done in a tactful and consistent way, this keeps communication open. Even quick prayers show the children where our heart is and makes them more aware of God's presence.

● I have come to realize the privilege and responsibility I have to pray for my children. Keeping a prayer notebook helps me focus daily on what to pray for and helps me feel organized in my prayer life. Organization is something I value in all other areas of my life, so why not in prayer too? I have a list of things I pray daily for my children, as well as for my husband and myself. This includes safety and protection, obedience to God, making good choices, and specific needs of the day. I also have seven different areas to pray about—one for each day of the week. These include:

- A burning desire for God, His Word, and prayer.
- Growth in graces such as compassion, kindness, and a giving spirit.
- Future spouses of my children.
- Their life work and goals.
- Relationships to peers, family, and authorities.
- Any specific personality traits that are proving troublesome.
- Talents and abilities.

Lamentations 2:19 (NIV) comes to mind as I pray: "Pour out your heart like water in the presence of the Lord. Lift up your hands to him for the lives of your children."

● We have kept a prayer journal with our children, writing down concerns they have, no matter how small. As they see evidence of God's work, we also record that. It is exciting for us to see how God honors our prayers.

● Whenever we are in the car and come upon a bad car accident, we pray aloud for the people hurt and for their families. I believe this gives my children a practical and proper response to frightening realities that they could otherwise feel helpless to do anything about. This teaches them that prayer is a good first response to a crisis.

● I knelt beside my three-year-old daughter's bed, thanking God for saving her from a near-drowning incident earlier in the day. She said her usual prayers that evening, and when she finished, I said, "Ruth, why don't you thank God for watching over you today at the picnic?" She began again, praying, "Dear God, thank You for watching over me today at the picnic . . . except for the one time You forgot me in the water." I explained to her that God was the only one who never took His eyes off of her and that He had provided a man to see her and rescue her. She understood and thanked God again.

● I have a friend I call once a week, and we pray together over the telephone. We don't even see each other that much, but the spiritual connection is so important. We share, pray, and keep each other accountable.

● Our whole family prays together each night. We begin with special prayers, Bible quotes, or bits of wisdom from books or daily calendars written for children. Sometimes we look up passages in the Bible. We then say a familiar prayer that we use often for thanking and praising God, ending with our own special prayers, petitions, or thanks. Some of the children's material that we have particularly liked include:

- *My Family's Prayer Calendar* (Shirley Dobson and Pat Verbal, Gospel Light).
- *God's Little Instruction Book for Kids* (Honor Books).
- *Bedtime Prayers for Little Ones* (Joni Eareckson Tada, Garborg's Heart 'n Home).

32

Pregnancy and Childbirth

I don't know about you, but when I was expecting my three children (not all at once), I loved reading books on pregnancy—especially individual stories of labor and delivery. Would my experience be similar? I wondered. At the end of my first pregnancy, the amniotic sac broke on midnight of the due date, and Chad was born six hours later. The second time around, the doctor broke the sac, and Nathan was born two hours later. Since the first two children came so quickly, I was convinced the third would be born after I sneezed. But Jordan was different. He was sitting head up in the womb with his legs crossed, so the doctors decided he would be born cesarean. That wasn't all bad. The first two times I worked hard while the hospital staff watched and waited. The third time, they worked hard while *I* watched and waited.

I've listened to lots of childbirth stories, but the most interesting I've heard to date is that of my cousin, Kathy, who unexpectedly delivered her second child in the hallway of her home! One week shy of her due date, Kathy began experiencing regular contractions. She waited through one

211

whole day of contractions, but since she was in no pain, she went to bed for the night. When she woke up at 4 A.M. the contractions were getting intense, although still not painful. Calling the doctor's office, she was instructed to come to the hospital.

After waking her husband, Mark, and calling her mom, Kathy showered. (Showering is a typical ritual for the woman in labor. I even took time to paint my nails!) The contractions were now coming hard and fast, and while getting out of the shower, her water bag broke. Sensing that the birth was imminent, she yelled to Mark, "Call 911!" and then collapsed in the hallway. She tells me that at that point inner panic had set in because she *knew* she was going to have the baby right there. Kathy's mom had just arrived, so she and Mark tried to make Kathy as comfortable (comfortable?) as possible.

When a paramedic walked in the door and realized her contractions were one minute apart, he confidently announced that the baby would be born right there! Really? Three pushes and Brianna was born right outside her sister Kristina's bedroom. After Mark woke Kristina to show her the new baby, Kathy and the newborn rode in an ambulance to the hospital.

Back at the house, Grandma suggested that Kristina call Grandpa and tell him that her baby sister had just been born right outside her bedroom door. She did. Grandpa thought he'd better talk to Grandma to get the *real* story. "That *was* the real story," Grandma exclaimed with a laugh.

Pregnancy is an exciting time. It's the beginning of a long adventure called parenting. But it can also be frightening to the woman who is not familiar with the nine-month process. For helpful advice on pregnancy, I turned to Juli Painter, R.N., presently working for an obstetrician. Together Juli and I worked at coming up with information that we think any pregnant woman should be aware of.

Emotionally, I Feel Like I'm on a Roller Coaster—Is That Normal?

Yes, a hundred times yes!

Not only do emotions erupt without warning, but they also can shift from one extreme to the other with mystifying speed. There is actually a logical, biological reason for this emotional turmoil. During the first trimester, our minds must adjust to the increase in hormone levels that enables our bodies to support and sustain the pregnancy. Some women are more sensitive to these changes than others, especially those who are sensitive to a similar hormonal shift prior to menstruation. If you suffer weepiness or edginess around your period, you may experience a comparable emotional instability as your body adjusts to the hormonal upheaval that comes with early pregnancy. Though you may feel overwhelmed by your thoughts now, expressing them and working them out will ease your transition to parenthood.[35]

What Are Some Constructive Ways to Deal with My Mood Swings?

(Taken from Healthy Pregnancy, Spring 1996)

- Be sure to sleep enough; you may need several more hours nightly.
- Avoid consuming excess sugar and caffeine, as these substances can give you a rush of energy followed by a low period, thereby worsening the mood shifts.
- Keep, or stay, fit. This will increase stamina and emotional well-being. Look into appropriate activities for pregnant women.
- Keep a journal. Recording your feelings will help you understand them and feel in control.

Are There Any Ways to Help Control Morning Sickness?

"Morning" sickness can occur at any time of the day or night. To combat it, try:

- Avoiding strong smells (food, perfume).
- Eating smaller meals more often.
- Avoiding caffeinated drinks.
- Snacking on dry crackers.
- Getting up slowly in the morning.

What Is the Best Way to Take Care of My Unborn Baby?

The best way a mom can take care of an unborn baby is to take care of herself. We desire to see our children grow physically, spiritually, mentally, and emotionally, and so should we! Another aspect of caring for the unborn baby is seeking out the best prenatal care possible. Regular appointments with your doctor are crucial to having a healthy pregnancy.

Through physical examinations and diagnostic tests, a doctor monitors the baby's growth and helps ensure that the mother's body tolerates the pregnancy well. Problems can be identified as they arise and, if possible, corrected before they cause harm.[36]

Should I Breastfeed?

There's no right or wrong answer, but all the experts seem to suggest that if you can, breastfeeding is a great choice.

Mother's milk is the best food for a baby—easily digestible and packed with all the necessary nutrients in precisely the right proportions. You have ready and waiting—clean and at the proper temperature—the perfect food supply for your infant. Breast-fed babies have fewer infections due to the antibodies in breast milk, and though a child may become allergic to formula, it's almost impossible to become allergic to mother's milk. Beyond the physical benefits, there are powerful emotional ones for mother and baby. If you run into problems getting started, ask your doctor or hospital for a referral to a lactation specialist.[37]

One of the things Juli enjoyed most about breastfeeding was excusing herself from the hustle and bustle of activity, going off to a quiet room to nurse her baby, and relaxing and enjoying the special one-on-one time between mother and child.

When Do Most Moms Begin Wearing Maternity Clothes?

Many start between the twelfth and sixteenth weeks, but I (Ellen) began much earlier. Some women like to hold out until the last possible moment, but since I can't stand wearing clothes that feel tight, in my first pregnancy I started wearing them around the tenth week, and by my third pregnancy I was wearing them at seven weeks. Begin wearing them when you get uncomfortable with your regular clothes.

Juli suggests that during these special months a pregnant mom needs to look and feel her best. Finances might be a little tight, and a lot of moms can't afford a wardrobe of new maternity clothes. Borrow clothes from a friend, look for resale shops, and go to garage sales. Garage sales abound in maternity clothes; you might have to hit quite a few to get everything you need, but the prices are great!

Should I Sign Up for Childbirth Classes?

Definitely! Juli strongly recommends that expectant moms (with their husbands) sign up for childbirth classes during the first pregnancy.

Anxiety about childbirth may take hold as the end of your term draws near. All sorts of thoughts are known to plague women at this vulnerable period—worries about tolerating the pain of labor, losing control, embarrassing themselves, encountering a medical emergency or "failing" in some way.

Education reduces the fear of the unknown. Many women and their labor partner participate in childbirth-preparation classes and find that these sessions are a valuable way to minimize worries, maximize confidence and build parenting skills. Practicing breathing techniques and methods of relaxation, exploring the various options for pain medication, and familiarizing yourself with the hospital setup and procedures will demystify the experience.[38]

Any Suggestions on What to Do on Those Nights Late in the Pregnancy When I Can't Fall Asleep?

- Read Psalm 139.
- Pray for your unborn child and family.
- Read a book of Bible meditations for pregnant mothers.
- Organize the shower gifts you have received to date.
- Bring the baby book up to date.
- Purchase a book of lullabies, and memorize ten or twenty to sing to the new baby during those late-night feedings yet to come.

33

Responsibilities and Chores

In order to realize success in the area of chores and children, the following ingredients must be included in the recipe:

Consistency

Simply said, if the parents aren't consistent, the kids won't be either.

Have a Plan

Some families' way of handling this might be simple, some might be more involved, but we all need a plan. If we aim at nothing, that's exactly what we'll hit.

Obedience Brings Affirmation

I've never believed that a child's obedience should be taken for granted. But if it's affirmed, there will be more obedience in the future!

Rally the Troops

Sometimes in our family we had an especially busy week that required extra help from each family member. On those occasions, I sat down at the kitchen table and made a list of everything that needed to be done. I then divided up the jobs among family members, wrote each person's tasks on a 3 x 5 card, and handed them all out. I also requested that the jobs be completed by a certain time. When possible, we celebrated afterwards with pie or ice cream!

Example of Parents

If the mother is a couch potato, she won't be successful at getting the child to work. Working *together* is a wonderful way to get a child moving.

Set expectations

If we're asking a child to clean his or her bedroom, it's helpful to state what we expect. Clear a path from the door to the closet? Vacuum and dust? Get all the dirty laundry out from under the bed? Be specific.

Ideas from Other Moms

● I have divided my housework into daily chores. Monday it's the kitchen, Tuesday it's the bathrooms, etc. I have also determined *simple* chores for the kids to do in that day's room(s). I put each day's jobs on an index card, and the cards go up on the refrigerator each day. This way the kids know what is expected of them and can feel that they are making a contribution to the family. My

218

older daughter (nine) enjoys the plan. I'm still working on consistency, but at least I feel like things are a little more under control.

● In an attempt to get a consistent chore routine for my ten- and eleven-year-old children, we let them split the list of chores into two lists, then alternate them weekly. The problem with this was soon evident: "It's not my week for that" . . . "I did that chore last week." I ended up doing the chores myself! Now we have a new plan that is actually working. I have a two-sided magnet on the refrigerator, with a child's name on each side. Whenever I need help, I ask the child whose name is on the magnet. Then I flip the magnet to the sibling's name. The kids love it.

● Responsibility is a valued quality in our home. As a child shows herself to be responsible, she receives more privileges, which of course carry with them more responsibility! This is very much connected to trust; if we don't trust our children, we won't give them responsibility. As they see that we do trust them, they will meet the challenge and become more responsible than we ever imagined!

● My philosophy on general housework is that it is not children's responsibility but mine. However, it is my goal with each of my four children that they be taught *how* to do all the chores that will someday be *their* responsibility. Before they leave home they will know how to clean house, do laundry, cook, and do yard work; but it will never be work they must do weekly for me.

● In our home, the children are responsible for their bedrooms. We announced when they were three that when they turned four they would begin making their beds. As they got older, I taught them how to clean and organize their rooms. At the beginning we did it *together*.

● Responsibility can be fun and can be learned at a young age. I keep a chore chart on the refrigerator, and as chores are completed, the children receive stars or smiley-face stickers to display their progress. At the end of the week they are rewarded by receiving an allowance based on the chart results.

● My son is the "king of dawdlers" when it comes to doing his small list of daily chores. Although he is just beginning to read, I find that he is much more motivated to complete his tasks if I give him a written to-do list each morning. He enjoys checking off the completed tasks and feels important.

● Responsibility and chores go hand in hand. I have two older sisters and one younger brother. My sisters and I each had certain chores that were to be done every Saturday (mine was dusting!). We also took turns setting the table and doing dishes. My brother was never given any responsibilities because he was the long-awaited son. As an adult, he cannot hold a job for more than a few months and has little respect for my parents. This is why I believe that having even small chores when a person is young can help toward becoming a responsible adult. As soon as our son could play with toys, I had him sit and watch me clean up at the end of the day. Now that he knows where his toys and books go and is able to put some of his things away himself, he is expected to do so. Since at this point he loves to help Mommy and Daddy, now is the perfect time to encourage a little responsibility.

● The rule in our house is simple: Chores for the week have to be done before weekend plans can be made.
　　I strongly believe that every member of the family must pitch in and help with all aspects of work around our house if the family is to function smoothly and if the children are

to feel needed and appreciated. From the time my children could undress themselves, they were taught that clothes go into the hamper when they are removed. The same goes for towels. This has probably made for some extra laundry over the years, but it has also made for a sense of order in our lives and much neater bedrooms and bathrooms.

- When my boys were small, we worked hard at keeping their bedrooms straightened up and their beds made. We had lists, check marks, and rewards. It was nice for me and the boys, around junior-high age, when I decided that their rooms were entirely up to them. I released all responsibility to them as long as they kept their door closed. I decided that other battles were more worthy of my attention.

- From first grade on, during the summer months my kids expect that they will *work* for two hours every day. *Work* includes practicing a musical instrument, cleaning their room, and doing other household jobs. The challenge for me as a mom is to make up the list and have plenty of jobs from which they can choose.

- Once our children started school, we spent the early part of each summer vacation discussing all the jobs that are necessary to be done in a household and decided together which jobs each child could do on a daily basis, a weekly basis, and a monthly basis. They started performing them during the summer, so that they were in the habit by the time school started. Each summer more jobs were added to their number. Sometimes they retained a particular job that they really liked or were good at; other times some of the jobs were rotated on a yearly basis. In that way they became used to being contributing members of our household at an early age.

34

siblings

When I think of siblings, I have a warm feeling in my heart because I am fond of my brother, Dave, and my sisters, Gail and Barb. Oh, sure, we had our share of fights and squabbles, but the rules our parents wisely set down were clear—basically, treat one another with respect. I enjoy getting together with my brother and sisters and rehashing the "remember when" stories.

"Remember when Mom used to leave for Ladies Missionary evenings at church once a month, and as soon as her car was out of the driveway Dad would say, 'Turn off all the lights, and we'll play hide and seek in the dark!'?" (Mom always wanted us to keep the lights *on.*)

A more frightening remembrance was Gail's serious injury, a brain concussion and skull fracture when she fell off a ten-foot slide onto concrete. We kids witnessed the prayers and concern of lots of folks, and we were grateful for God's healing in that situation.

"Remember the nightmares Barb used to have about *ladybugs*?" (I recently saw a Beanie Baby stuffed ladybug in a local gift shop and bought it for her!)

"Remember how Dave, at four or five, used to go out in the backyard, stand on top of the garbage can, wave his arms, and sing loudly enough for the whole neighborhood to hear, 'I'm Popeye the Sailor Man, I live in a garbage can'?"

Siblings share experiences and moments throughout the fabric of their lives that have the potential to create special bonds or to cause unhealthy competition and sometimes even pain. I believe parents are the overseers of this task. If siblings are taught mutual respect while they're growing up at home, the fond bonds pay off in the long run.

Ideas from Other Moms

● Our two daughters both prefer sitting in the front seat of the car. To make things equitable, one daughter sits in the front seat of the car Monday, Wednesday, and Friday, while the other one gets the privilege Tuesday, Thursday, and Saturday. We also use this system to decide who practices piano first on the same days.

● We have two boys who are a year and a half apart. The older was and is a good example and role model. His younger brother always tried so hard to be like his brother and to imitate whatever he did. The older brother never seemed to come in second or copy the younger brother. I didn't realize that bothered the younger one until his older brother broke out with the dreaded childhood spots to which they had both been exposed and the younger brother said, "I can't even get the chicken pox first!" Since that early childhood day, we have had a heightened awareness of the need for each of the kids to have their own identity and the opportunity to do something that no family member before them has done.

● Our boys have been known to carry on some rip-roaring fights. One argument took place while they were at the grocery store with my husband. He marched the boys outside to the car, putting the younger in front and the elder in the back. Somewhere between one door and the other my husband heard loud *wailing*. The younger claimed he had been "slugged" in the head when Dad wasn't looking. The older one flatly denied the charge. My husband gave them a lecture on honesty and then asked for the story again. Both maintained the same story. He calmly said, "If you both say you are telling the truth, then I must believe you. I know that neither one of you would lie to your dad. I trust my boys to tell the truth."

Later that evening after we had put both boys to bed, we heard sobbing coming from the older boy's bedroom. In a broken voice, he confessed and asked his dad's forgiveness (and eventually his brother's). My husband's words to me were, "Every once in a while God shows me that *calmness* is the wisest route."

We are trying to teach our kids to honor and respect each other. As our kids get older, we notice that the teasing, sarcasm, and egging each other on seems cool to them. We as parents want our family to be a safe place for each of us to be comfortable enough to talk about what's important to us—our thoughts and feelings. Here's an example: Our family was planning on going to a school roller-skating party. Our oldest son was asking that we keep the younger siblings at home, because at previous parties they had teased him about skating with girls. What we encouraged him to do was to say to his siblings, "Guys, I'm probably going to be talking to girls at the family roller-skating party. Please don't bug me and tease me." We want our kids to be able to say honestly what they need, and we want the rest of the family to respond with respect and understanding. Too many families use teasing and sarcasm to express underlying anger without dealing with the *real* feelings and issues.

● I feel it's important to keep peace between siblings. When we have a problem between children and someone is at fault, we ask them to say "I'm sorry, _____," and the other is asked to respond with "I forgive you" and a hug.

● During the years our son was undergoing treatment for childhood leukemia, it became important to have time alone with our two daughters. Special lunches or outings to answer their questions and quiet their spirits were helpful in dealing with their fears. Honesty and open conversation were encouraged by us as parents. We are grateful for the good health of our son, and we are also thankful that we kept up with our daughters.

● Our three daughters shared a bedroom until our oldest was fourteen. In their early years this was a necessity. When we had more room, we still thought it was best for them—so they could bond, share, and care for each other.

● On the occasions that we left an older sibling home to babysit younger siblings, we agreed to pay them *all* if they all worked together and got along well. If they squabbled and fought, nobody earned anything!

● My firstborn has never been attracted to toys. As a baby she never played with the busybox in her crib or playpen, though she adored pillows and large stuffed animals. As she grew, she was attracted to paper, pencils, and bags. In addition, any kitchen utensil was fascinating to her. I used to wonder why they made toys for kids! Then I had child #2! Every toy that child #1 ignored was now played with constantly. Toys drew her like a magnet. As a thrifty mom, it gave me a lot of pleasure to see those toys that cost so much get used, but I also learned a valuable lesson. We can assume nothing about what's *normal* for a child. Even a choice as simple as "Will my child like toys?" is unpredictable and will vary widely from child to child. This has helped me be open-handed with my children's preferences as they grow in other areas of their lives.

- When I had a toddler at home and brought home a newborn (which happened several times because I had five children), I made a Toddler and Baby Book with the toddler. On the left side of the page we put photos of the toddler eating, playing, or sleeping, and on the right side of the page we put photos of the baby eating, playing, or sleeping. These books were perfect to pull out while I was nursing the baby, because it was *affirming* to the toddler.

- My twin son and daughter were in the same afternoon kindergarten class. One morning I heard my daughter say to my son, "How 'bout if we go to school this afternoon and pretend that we don't know each other!"

- At four and a half, our second child was tired of being bullied by her six-year-old sister. One day I heard her preaching her own theology to my older daughter: "If you don't share, God's going to spank you. When you get to heaven, God will open the book and read, 'YOU HAVE TO SHARE!'"

- My junior-high daughter has proudly begun shaving her legs. Our five-year-old daughter watched her in wonder one night. Later she asked my husband, "How come Sister sharpens her legs with that pink thing?"

35

Single Moms

~~~◦◦◦~~~

The circumstance that brought Shelley, Linda, Nancy, and Rose together is that of single motherhood. It's not what they had wanted or expected, and it's caused deep feelings of pain. For some, the pain seemed as bad as death. As I interviewed these women, I learned that they shared common experiences—their husbands had had compulsive affairs, behaviors, and fantasies; each of these moms had been lied to; they'd received anger and blame when they confronted their husbands about irrational behavior; they'd all seen selfishness, adultery, and husbands who didn't like dealing with the reality of consequences. This is not the case with all single moms, but sadly, for a large number it is.

As painful as all four of their stories were, these moms said that when the truth of their situations came out, it was somewhat therapeutic, because they were no longer wondering, Where is he? Who's he with? What's he spending money on? Will he come through on his promise this time? Of course, the challenge when the truth surfaced was, "Where do we go from here?" Once they knew the truth, they had to make tough decisions and appropriate changes, no longer tolerating the consistently destructive behavior of their husbands. When the initial shock and pain of their situations moved from "critical" to "stable," these four moms made the choice to be the best single parents they could be. According to Dr. Fitzhugh Dodson, the challenge of single parenting is "not to neglect your children, but to make sure that you take care of yourself, too."[39]

As I talked about all this with Shelley, who heads up the single moms' group at our church, some of the challenges to single parenting that surfaced were: loneliness, finding resources for support, dealing with the ex-husband, finances, visiting arrangements for kids, and forgiveness. I chose to get together with the four single moms mentioned above, discussing these topics for the benefit of other single mothers who are dealing with similar challenges. The question/answer format that follows is the result of my meetings with these moms. I hope this chapter will be a helpful balance between reality and hope for any mother reading it.

How Do You Deal with Loneliness?

These four ladies acknowledged that they miss male companionship but said that the most painful loneliness for them was the pain of a lonely marriage. Although previously they felt trapped, they now are experiencing freedom to grow. One mom commented that she is grateful to be part of a supportive group of single moms, whereas before there was no bad marriage group. In each mom's situation, her circle of friends has changed considerably. Where they used to get together with couples, it is now much more comfortable to go out with other women or groups of women. All of the moms I spoke with have supportive extended families whom they have appreciated greatly.

It's harder to let go of the kids when you're a single parent, they admitted. As the kids get older and have their own schedules, the potential for loneliness in single moms is greater. They joke together about making appointments in advance with their counselors for the years when they reach the empty nest. But all four moms also agree that a single mom only has to be lonely if she chooses to go it alone. Moving on includes making new friendships and finding ways to have fun and be healthy.

What Have Been Your Most Helpful Resources for Support?

These women strongly stated that it is unwise to attempt single motherhood alone. Divorce Recovery Workshops have been extremely beneficial, especially when they're presented in a woman's home church. It feels affirming and validating when the church cares about her situation. Support groups offer the opportunity to meet other moms. When Shelley, Linda, Nancy, and Rose first visited support groups, they were in a state of mind in which they wondered if they'd ever make it. Their wounds and pain were fresh, and anger and bitterness were not far beneath the surface. They found it encouraging to see other single moms who seemed to have some order to their lives, who were happy and able to laugh again. Support groups do require effort to get plugged in—many women visit only once; but if there is a commitment to coming, there can be growth and change as the moms encourage, challenge, and empathize with one another. It's comforting to meet other single moms who have tackled difficult issues and lived through them.

Each mom concurred that establishing a relationship with a good Christian counselor is constructive over the long term, especially when it comes to dealing with child-raising issues. In regard to printed material, these four moms gave high ratings to *Single-Parent Family*, a monthly magazine published by Focus on the Family.

What Are Your Suggestions on How to Deal with an Ex-husband?

One reality of being a single parent is that although there's been a divorce, the relationship doesn't end. A husband and wife may divorce, but children don't divorce their father. Even in the case of total abandonment and no contact, there are still fear and resentment to deal with. Keeping kids' issues separate from marital issues is difficult, but it's a goal worth working toward. There's a difference between respecting an ex-husband and treating him with respect. The latter should not include being a doormat. Respecting one's own dignity, speaking the truth, and maintaining healthy boundaries while treating the ex-spouse with courtesy are essential.

Most of these single moms limit their conversations with their ex-husbands to business issues, calendars, and schedules. One mom and her ex-husband meet periodically to discuss ground rules for dealing with their teenagers. They work toward having agreed-on standards for things like curfews and movies. One of the tensions many single moms experience is that the kids feel comfortable to yell, scream, and talk back at Mom's house because it's *home*. They consider it a safe place to let it all hang out. They don't often try these things at Dad's house for a couple of reasons. One is that they're *visiting*, and the second is that Dad is often the one who provides money for them to do some of the extra things they like to do, and they don't want to jeopardize that relationship. In spite of all the issues that prompted a divorce, all four moms agreed that working toward being allies with the ex-spouse is a worthy goal. This provides much more security for the children over the years.

What's It Like When Your Kids Leave for the Weekend to Stay with Their Dad?

Unanimously, moms said that the first time their kids went to stay with ex-husbands for a visit, the moms cried. At the beginning it was also difficult for the children, because they felt as though they were abandoning their moms. These moms suggest planning ahead to change the weekend from an awful time to a fun time. Shelley cleans house on Thursday nights, so the weekend can be spent doing dinner and a movie with a friend or a little shopping. Linda said that during the weekends that her triplets stay with her ex-husband, she reads something about child-care, so that even though she's not *with* them, she's doing something *for* them. All the moms said that as much as they miss the children when they're gone, they try to enrich their own lives and find time to have fun on those weekends, which contributes to their being better moms in the long run.

What's Your Biggest Challenge Regarding Finances?

Hands down, all four moms said the biggest challenge financially is that they are torn between the choice of excelling at work or excelling as a mom. They could all work more hours and have better jobs if they wanted, but they feel a strong need to be around for the children as much as possible. Some of these moms have turned down jobs with higher pay when those jobs would have taken more time away from their children. As I listened to their conversations, I realized that God has honored this in all four situations. These moms are a tribute to the principle that as they have made good choices, God has given them their daily bread.

Would You Share Some Thoughts on Forgiveness?

- It's not unusual to feel that "I don't want to forgive because he doesn't deserve it."
- It's difficult to forgive when there's been no shame or changed behavior.
- I have to forgive in order to have a healthy relationship with God and others, and in order to live with dignity as opposed to anger and resentment.
- If I get stuck in bitterness, I can't realize God's new blessings.
- No matter how painful it is to forgive, it's right, and it's not worth holding on to old offenses and growing into a bitter old woman.
- Forgiveness allows disconnecting; otherwise a woman stays dependent on her ex-husband.
- If I don't forgive, the offender controls me.
- After forgiving, I gained back control of my emotions, and that enhanced the spirit of my home!
- Typically, the kids' forgiveness happens later than the moms'; so it's good for the kids to have a role model in the mother.
- Don't think of forgiving *everything* at once. Break things down. Forgiveness is a *process* and an *attitude*.
- Forgiveness does not mean living the same way as before—falling back into unhealthy patterns. There's a difference between forgiveness and trust.
- One mom who was having trouble with forgiveness prayed for her ex-husband, and then she prayed that someday she would *mean* it. She realized that her feelings wouldn't always be caught up with her actions.

After spending time with Shelley, Linda, Nancy, and Rose, it became obvious that they had all been through substantial pain. Yet it was also obvious that significant healing has been taking place in their souls. One mom shared how she recently received $1,000, totally unexpectedly, because the IRS had made a mistake and gave her a refund. That was a terrific example to her children of how God provides. Another mom had been asked the question, at a gathering of single moms, "If you could do anything you wanted, what would it be?" She answered, "Be an interior designer!" The person she was speaking with ended up hiring her to work for a decorating company she owned! Another mom with triplets is grateful for *her* mom, who baby-sits for the three little ones. Also, she couldn't have handpicked a better job. She teaches part-time now while her triplets are toddlers, but her hours will increase as the children get older. When moms put their children as a priority, God does provide.

When the elders and leaders at our church realized there was a need for a single moms' support group, they approached Shelley about leading one. Being asked was affirming for Shelley, plus it continues to meet needs in other women's lives. As I heard these accounts, there was a redemptive fragrance in the room, as is so often the case when individuals see that God can use suffering as a launching pad for glorification.

Not all single moms are single because their husbands left them. Years ago my friend Brenda's husband was killed by a disgruntled employee, which left her with the responsibility of raising her two sons, twelve and ten, alone. Not long after Dale died, Brenda wrote some thoughts about a single mom from the Bible, which I asked permission to include in this book. I'm glad she agreed, because it's a great story for all of us to be reminded of, especially moms without husbands. Here are Brenda's words:

Because of Dale's death, the story about Elisha and the widow (2 Kings 4:1–7, NIV) has become one of my favorite Bible stories.

The wife of a man from the company of the prophets
cried out to Elisha, "Your servant my husband is
dead, and you know that he revered the Lord."
VERSE 1A

233

I like how the widow said that statement. It reminds me of things I've said to God. "How could you let Dale die? You know that he revered You. He was doing everything right, and You still let him die. Now, we are Your responsibility. How are You going to provide for us?"

> "But now his creditor is coming
> to take my two boys as his slaves."
> VERSE 1B

The widow had two sons, and I have two sons. She felt the responsibility, the joy, and the sorrow of providing for her two boys.

I thank God that I do not have collection agents knocking at my door, requiring me to pay them with money I do not have. God has provided for my financial needs. The creditor that I fear is the evil influences of this world. Dale was a buffer for us, shielding us from those evil influences. He was so good, so honest, so full of integrity, so strong and conservative, and he was fun too. Now who will be the protector of these two boys?

I love Elisha's gentle, kind reply. I love it that there were no reprimands. He didn't say, "You seem to be feeling angry. Would you like to tell me more about what you are feeling?" He didn't say, "I've read about grief stages, and I know where you are." He didn't say, "You need to trust God more." He didn't say, "Look, this is your opportunity to become a strong woman." Notice Elisha's humble, gentle, kind reply:

> Elisha replied to her, "How can I help you?
> Tell me, what do you have in your house?"
> VERSE 2A

It seems as if Elisha is asking, "What are your assets?" or "What do we have to work with?" It reminds me of God's question to Moses in Exodus 4:2, "What is that in your hand?" I like the question, "What do you have in your house?" It is special to me for several reasons. When Dale died, we had only been in our house for two and a half weeks. I'm so glad we had moved in. I like our home, and I want to use it for God's business. I feel like God gave it to us to use for Him. Thinking about that question has often been the impetus I needed to invite guests for dinner or to open my house to use for meetings or overnight guests. Sometimes I invite guests over on the spur of the moment. Then I smile at that question, "What do you have in your house?" I guess that I also think a home is more important to me than it was to Dale. I like to think that Elisha understood that, and God understands that, and He doesn't condemn it or deny it but sensitively asks a hidden challenge—"How will you use your home?"

Several years ago I read the series of books about Anne of Green Gables. Anne quite often would meet someone for the first time and sense that he or she was a kindred spirit. That has happened with me as well on occasion. The first time I met and spoke with my dear friend Ellie Kniffen, I knew she was a kindred spirit. I think the widow in this story is a kindred spirit as well. Remembering Elisha's question, "What do you have in your house?" notice this dear widow's response:

> "Your servant has nothing there at all," she said.
> VERSE 2B

I loved it when I read that she said, "Nothing . . . at all." I have often in self-pity said, "I have nothing at all left. I am totally bereft. I don't even have any choices left." Then when I pause to be reasonable and stop my pity party, I say, "Forgive me, Lord, for the sin of self-pity. I do have so much left. My assets—my sons, my friends, You, the Lord Jesus, my finances, my church, my neighbors, and much, much more—are great." I then count my blessings and say, "Thank You, Jesus." After thinking just briefly, the widow too remembered that she had something.

> "Your servant has nothing there at all," she said,
> "except a little oil."
> VERSE 2B

Following this, Elisha gave the widow specific instructions on what to do:

> Elisha said, "Go around and ask all your neighbors for empty jars. Don't ask for just a few. Then go inside and shut the door behind you and your sons. Pour oil into all the jars, and as each is filled, put it to one side." She left him and afterward shut the door behind her and her sons. They brought the jars to her and she kept pouring. When all the jars were full, she said to her son, "Bring me another one." But he replied, "There is not a jar left." Then the oil stopped flowing.
> VERSES 3–6

I like the fact that this widow had to ask for help. How embarrassing, how humiliating! I like the fact that she needed to ask for help from her neighbors—those close to her. I like the fact that she did not need just one jar from each neighbor, but as many as they could spare. I like the fact that she worked it out privately, in her home, with her door closed. I like the fact that her sons were needed and required to help her. I like the fact that her sons were allowed the privilege of seeing the power of God and God's provision for them.

> She went and told the man of God, and he said, "Go, sell the oil and pay your debts. You and your sons can live on what is left."
> VERSE 7

Isn't this the best part of the story? God not only provided for her debts, but He provided abundantly. The widow had enough to live on. I want very much to believe this for me and my sons as well.

I have several little oil lamps. As I light my lamps, I am reminded of this story and encouraged to trust God to be sufficient for all of my needs. I hope you will be encouraged in the same way.

BRENDA S. ROWELL

36

Sons

To be a mother is the grandest vocation in the world.
No being has a position of such power and influence.
She holds in her hands the destiny of nations; for
to her is necessarily committed the making of the
nation's citizens. (Hannah Whitall Smith)[40]

From the day that the first of our three sons was born, I
sensed the incredible privilege and responsibility of guiding the
first little fella that came into our family. Those same feelings
were present from the moment of birth with our second and
third sons as well. After many years of motherhood, the sense
of incredible privilege and responsibility is still there.

Raising three sons is not something I have done alone. My
husband and I share the adventure and are grateful for the positive influence of other family members, friends, and teachers.
But the main responsibility of overseeing their growth into
manhood is bestowed on us as parents. Some of the qualities
that I most want to see developed in all three of our sons are
honesty, kindness, reverence for God, and *purity*.

Honesty

Lies will get any man into trouble,
but honesty is its own defense.
PROVERBS 12:13

From the beginning, I chose to notice and celebrate acts of honesty that I saw in my sons. I like catching my kids doing things right! Here's an example that happened in our house. Jordan (nine) called Nathan (fifteen) an unkind name. Because we don't like name-calling around our house. I told Jordan that for that offense, he would not be allowed to touch his gerbils or cat for two days (a painful consequence for Jordan). Halfway through the second day, Jordan came to me and apologetically said that he had forgotten the two-day rule and had been playing with the cat that morning. Instead of punishing him for breaking the rule, I thanked him for his honesty, reminding him not to play with the animals for the rest of the day. He walked away at peace, reinforced for having told the truth. To have extended more punishment would have been unreasonable; it seemed much wiser to reward his honesty. We have practiced this same principle with all three sons and are enjoying the trust we have in them.

Kindness

Your own soul is nourished when you are kind;
it is destroyed when you are cruel.
PROVERBS 11:17

When you deliver a meal to a friend in need, how do you feel when you're walking away from her house? I feel great (consider the word in this proverb—"*nourished*"). When we see our children doing something kind for a sibling or a friend, it is so important to affirm them for their good choice. When they make a poor choice (and we all do from time to time), calmly

238

pointing it out and discussing the hurt caused to the other person as well as the hurt caused to ourselves is important.

Reverence for God

For the reverence and fear of God are basic to all wisdom.
Knowing God results in every other kind of understanding.
PROVERBS 9:10

Just as a house needs a foundation, so does a family. Psalm 119:165 holds out the promise that "those who love your laws have great peace of heart and mind and do not stumble." The security for a child who sees that his parents believe *and* practice reverence for God and His Word is immeasurable. We try to remind our boys that God will bless them with wisdom as they reverence Him.

Purity

Don't let anyone think little of you because you
are young. Be their ideal; let them follow the way
you teach and live; be a pattern for them in your
love, your faith, and your clean thoughts.
1 TIMOTHY 4:12

To be pure is to be unsoiled and unblemished. In order to guide our sons toward purity, we are responsible to make a lot of good choices *for* them when they are young. What will we let them look at? Listen to? Who will we let them be around? Where will we take them? As they grow older, we give them increasing freedom, but not without continued instruction. As they mature and are out and about on their own, we still caution them about situations they are likely to encounter.

In particular, sexual impurity is a destructive force in our society today, and as 1 Timothy 4:12 teaches, purity begins in the mind. From the time my boys were young, I talked a good deal with them about their personal responsibility in making choices for purity. It's not usually one major blunder that messes up a person's life—it's a string of small choices that lead up to it.

Just as the small choices our sons make each day are important to building their character, so are ours. We sometimes forget how much clout we have in our sons' lives. In order to be women with positive influence, *we* need to be women of *honesty*, *kindness*, *reverence for God*, and *purity* ourselves.

Being godly mothers of sons is a high calling! I found it interesting that of the two original poems submitted by mothers for this book, *both* of them were written about sons!

Ideas from Other Moms

My Three Sons
(Dedicated to Nathan, Chris, and Lucas)
by Deborah W. Grobe

Muddy shoes, grass-stained pants,
Excited finds of Spring's first ants.

Boys and soccer balls in constant motion,
For me all these things evoke emotion.

Sand in toes and wind-tangled hair,
Ocean's beauty everywhere.

Crabbing, fishing, gathering sea treasures,
Playing board games in rainy weather.

Jumping in leaves and at scary faces,
Family hikes to quiet places.

Eager mornings off to school,
Frantic days and endless car pools.

Tracked-in snow and wet snow clothes,
Rosy cheeks, a runny nose,

Building snowmen and sliding down hills,
With thoughts like this my heart thrills.

All year 'round you bring such pleasure,
Memories that I will always treasure.

Even the rough times have hidden joys,
For this lucky mother of three wonderful boys.

Before the Birth of My Son
by Terri Bradford, 1996

Before the birth of my son . . .
I took for granted having time to get ready in the morning.

And knew nothing about having to change my clothes
because they had been smeared with pureed banana.

I took for granted cleaning my house
and having it stay that way.

And knew nothing about stray Cheerios
crunching under my feet.

I took for granted my size 6 dress.

But never had a pair of size 3½ Nikes
waiting on my staircase.

I took for granted the pats on my back
from my colleagues at work.

But never felt the warmth of the gentle pats
from my son's little hand.

I took for granted the time I had to make phone calls.
And knew nothing of how it felt to be called "Mama."

I took for granted the luxury
of sleeping in on a Saturday morning.

And knew nothing of the joy I would feel
in seeing his morning smile from the crib.

I took for granted sleeping through the night.

But missed out on the opportunity to pray
in the stillness of a midnight feeding.

I understood that God sent His Son because He loved us,
But didn't know just how much until He gave me my son.

● While raising my sons, I try to remember that I am also raising someone's husband. My mother-in-law did a great job of preparing her son to be a wonderful husband. I pray that our boys will be the same kind of godly, caring husbands that their dad is. I've taught them how to do laundry, iron, mend, vacuum, clean bathrooms, and wash dishes. They are adept at diapering and bathing babies. They can cook everything from homemade bread and pies to chicken parmesan. As a culture, we spend a great amount of effort educating and preparing our sons for their careers. I think being a good husband is equally important, and in some ways a more difficult task. My husband bears the major responsibility of modeling the role of the husband, but I have enjoyed teaching homemaking skills to my sons so they can be encouraging to their wives someday.

● My younger of two sons, Brad, found the book *How to Raise Boys to Become Men* by our couch where I had been reading the night before. He walked into the kitchen and said, with a smirk on his face, "*How to Raise Boys to Become Men*, huh?" I said, "I can use all the help I can get, don't you agree?" He paused a bit as if thinking and then said, "Well actually, I think *I'm* doing OK, but you could probably use some help with Andy."

⬤ Gardening is one of the most gratifying things I do with my boys. Each spring I take them shopping to pick out seeds and bedding plants. I make most of the choices, but I let them make a few too. (They are typically a bit unorthodox—giant sunflowers!) I let them get involved in the ground preparation and planting. They make a daily ritual (without my prompting) of checking on our vegetable garden. They also have little garden baskets to carry their booty back to the house. It is hard to express how much they enjoy being involved in all of this. It has also been a great way to instill a love of nature and an awe for God's handiwork, as well as helping them see that hard work does pay you back.

⬤ When my sons were in grade school, shortly after we had moved into our new home, I unknowingly locked the house keys inside the house before we walked over to the school for the annual book fair. I had my purse and some money with me, as we were planning to make purchases at the fair. My husband was at a business meeting in Chicago and would not return home until 11 P.M. When the boys and I realized we were locked out for the evening, we walked to a nearby restaurant, enjoyed a quiet meal, and read our books. We talked about school and activities for several hours. It was such an enjoyable evening—no phone, no TV, no car or other activities to distract us. I fondly remember all the time we had to share and talk with each other that night. When it was dark, we walked back to the house and slept in the car until Dad got home. When I remember the adventure we shared and the family time we enjoyed together, I have thought about "accidentally" locking my keys in the house again!

⬤ Teenage boys talk and open up when they are fed delicious food and given undivided attention. Every other month or so, I take my teenage sons out to eat, one at a time. They choose the restaurant. I ask lots of questions and give lots of affirmation. I tell them what I like about them and nice things I've heard others say about them. When a couple of months have gone by, they'll often say, "Isn't it about time for you to take me out to eat again?"

It was a beautiful summer morning. Chad (four) and I had just returned from the grocery store and unloaded the bags from the car. While my son finished a snack, we sat together on the back-porch steps. We were having one of those unhurried talks a mom never forgets. He wanted to know whom he was going to marry. I explained that was something I did not know—that it depended on women he met and choices he made, and that God could help him in that big decision. I asked him what kind of woman he thought he might *like* to marry. His response was amazing! "She has to love God and bake bread, and she has to be able to keep a secret!" After I affirmed him for his great thoughts, he confidently announced, "When I find her, I'm going to name her Bambi!"

My five-year-old and I recently went on a "date" to a concert and then out for ice cream. He enjoyed listening to a musical group and choosing where to eat afterwards. He had my undivided attention, and we talked about topics ranging from toys to school to how my husband and I decided to marry each other. I was amazed at what was going on inside his young mind. We make this a monthly outing.

One day I overheard my son, age four, having a conversation with his father. Erik said, "Daddy, you can fix anything, but Mommy can't fix anything." Not wanting to encourage this budding male chauvinist, my husband said, "That's not true, Erik. Your mom can fix lots of things." Erik thought about this for a moment and then commented, "Yeah, I guess you're right. Mommy can fix dinner!"

37

Spiritual Nurturing

~~~⚬~~~

$\mathcal{N}$ot until a Sunday morning Bible Instruction Class did I realize that I might see some truths about kids and spiritual nurturing in the Old Testament book of Ecclesiastes! But I did as chapter 7 came alive to me. The whole book of Ecclesiastes speaks of the wisdom of *balance* in our lives, and I believe it's important for us as parents to capture that idea with our children.

> See the way God does things and fall into line.
> Don't fight the facts of nature. Enjoy prosperity whenever
> you can, and when hard times strike, realize that God
> gives one as well as the other—so that everyone will realize
> that nothing is certain in this life.
> VERSES 13–14

My dad is a wise man. One of the principles he taught me when I was growing up is one I have kept alive with my children. On the occasions that I had trouble in a class at school and complained about the teacher, my dad always suggested, "Try to discover exactly what the teacher is looking for and go for it. *Fall in line* with his or her plan and you will do well."

Teaching our children to fall into line with their Creator's agenda is wise. When the good times come, give thanks and enjoy them—they are gifts. When the hard times come, remember that He is always with us.

> None who have faith in God will ever be disgraced
> for trusting him.
> PSALM 25:3

Ideas from Other Moms

● Some of the best opportunities I've had to talk to my kids about God is while we are performing life's tasks. It does say in Deuteronomy 6:5–7 (NIV), "Love the Lord your God with all your heart and with all your soul and with all your strength. These commandments that I give you today are to be upon your hearts. Impress them on your children. Talk about them when you sit at home and when you walk along the road, when you lie down and when you get up." So I talk with my children about God and about my own spiritual life with its ups and downs when we are in the car driving to school, peeling carrots for supper, or enjoying a sunset together. Children remember what parents have taught them about God in consistent, casual conversation.

● I try to remind myself that in everything I do, my children are aware of my actions and my reactions. This makes me realize that I need to stay in prayer, communicating with God throughout the day. I want my kids to know that it is God who helps me stay on the right path and helps me say, "I'm sorry."

● When my oldest son was four years old, our family took a trip home to New England. My youngest sister had just married, and her husband was in seminary. They both love camping, which my husband and I abhor! Uncle Gary asked my little son, "Would you like to camp out with me in Grandpa's field?" My son was *so* excited! Gary relates that about 10:30 that night he heard a little voice say, "Uncle Gary, is God with Mommy?" "Yes." Silence. "Uncle Gary, is God with us?" "Yes." Silence. "Oh, then there are *two* Gods!" Gary said that was his first real test as a pastor—explaining the omnipresence of God to a four-year-old.

● When at all possible, we have tried to serve together in church as a family, so that our kids look forward to service within God's community of believers. This has been in small ways, such as letting them help set up for choir or children's church or helping to serve a church dinner.

● My children learn about God from me, from the church, and from their own Bible discoveries; but I do feel that much can be learned about God through everyday life. In the storms we see God's power. In the beauty of spring we see newness of life and the hope of resurrection. In observing shallow root systems of a plant we can ask what kind of soil conditions we have in our own hearts.

● I strive to see my children from God's perspective, remembering that He created them as unique individuals. God specifically placed them in our care, knowing our strengths and weaknesses. Whether at any given moment we feel proud of or embarrassed by our children, we should be humbled before God, continually seeking His wisdom for guidance in raising them. This attitude is *especially* helpful during toddler and adolescent years!

● We celebrate the spiritual birthdays of our girls. We think it's important to remember the day they said yes to Jesus. I let them plan the menu for a special dinner. We usually have our favorite Buster Bar Torte for dessert. To the tune of "Happy Birthday," we sing:

Happy Birthday to you,
Only one will not do.
Born again means salvation,
We're glad you've had two!

I don't like to have presents or gifts at this celebration. I feel that our lives are gifts we give back to God.

I have an old quart canning jar filled with twenty walnuts and two cups of rice. The walnuts represent the things God would have us do, and the rice represents the fun things that we like to do. If we pour rice into the jar first, the walnuts will never fit. If we put the walnuts in the jar first, the rice poured over and around the nuts fits in just fine. The lesson, of course, is that if we put time with and for God before time for other things we want to do, we'll have plenty of time for both. If, however, we put the things we want to do first, we'll never fit time for God into our life.

I'm so thankful to know God as my heavenly Father. I need someone to lean on, cry out to, cling to at times—just like my children do with me. This has especially been true for me since both of my parents died. God is my counselor, my source of wisdom and love, and my security in an ever-changing world.

Deuteronomy 6:4–7 speaks of teaching our children about God in a natural way as we go through our day. I remember singing the same song to my daughter every morning when she was little: "This is the day, this is the day that the Lord has made. I will rejoice, I will rejoice and be glad in it." I reminded myself that I was raising a God-fearing, independent person, not just a baby. That helped me keep things in perspective.

My son has helped me gain a better understanding of God the Father. I am in awe of the love God must feel for

His people. As a parent, I would do anything to take away my son's pain when he cries. God's love and compassion are so much greater than anything humanly possible. Knowing how I feel when my son turns to me for comfort gives me a mere glimpse of how God must feel when we come to Him for comfort through our prayers. We cannot spare our children from the disappointments of this world, just as God cannot spare us. But knowing the love I feel for my son and how it mirrors what God feels for us, I am more aware of the strength of His comfort and steadfast love.

● We have included some elements of worship in our family time at home, explaining segments of the church service such as the Doxology, the Gloria Patri, the Apostles' Creed, Communion, baptism, and the Lord's Prayer. As a result, these parts of the service don't seem foreign or hard to understand when the child is old enough to participate.

● We had an interesting experience as a result of grief. My dad died three years ago, and Freddie's dad died a year ago. A couple of months after Freddie's dad's death, I was riding in our van with my son and daughter. The two children were in the backseat, and Carleigh was crying quietly. Judd told me she was upset, and I asked him to do what he could to comfort her. The resulting conversation was fascinating.

Judd: Carleigh, what's the matter?
Carleigh: I miss Grandpa, and I'm never going to be able to see him again.
Judd: Well, you'll get to see him again in heaven.
Carleigh: How do I know I'm going to heaven?
Judd: Well, you'll go to heaven when you die if you've accepted Jesus as your personal Savior.
Linda (interrupting): Judd, for her we call it "asking Jesus to be your best friend."

Judd: If you ask Jesus to be your best friend, then you'll go to heaven to be with Him when you die.

Carleigh: How do I ask Him to be my best friend?

Judd: You just pray.

Carleigh: What do I say?

He prayed with her, and when they finished, he assured her that now she could be sure she'd go to heaven when she died, and therefore she'd also be sure to see Grandpa. I was absolutely thrilled at this and thanked God as I was driving along!

Judd: There! Now, Carleigh, do you feel better?

Carleigh: No! I still miss Grandpa!

What happened in the van that day was a good example to me of how our Christianity is woven into our everyday lives. What a marvel—the physical death of Grandpa helped lead Carleigh into spiritual life!

We have used a little booklet since our kids were about two, entitled *Catechism for Young Children*. It goes over the basics about God and the Christian faith. It is in a typical catechism order with questions and answers. (Who made you? God. What else did God make? God made all things. Why did God make you and all things? For His own glory.) At first, it's a matter of memorizing and repeating memorized answers. Now that our kids are a little older, we have had many wonderful conversations about the meaning of the answers, and understanding has come.

If possible, before your children are born or when they are small, commit your family to a church or a fellowship of believers. From that time on, try to make your church the center of your social and service life. Support all activities, help with children's ministries, and be involved in adult groups. Your children will benefit beyond all your efforts.

They will have a group of people that care for their spiritual growth and well-being. I cannot begin to thank God for the adults He has sent into my children's lives as role models from our church. God has blessed us far beyond the time we have invested in our church.

Both of my sons were baptized at their request when they were eighth graders. We had a special cake made with a significant Bible verse on it. Then we invited about twelve people who had had an impact on the kids spiritually to watch them be baptized. Afterwards we came back to the house, and the son who was baptized received a new Bible. Each spiritual mentor gave a word of encouragement or a special verse and shared it with everyone, also writing it on the blank pages at the end of the Bible, signing and dating it.

38

Television

~⊙~

$\mathcal{M}$y husband and I rarely watch TV. Every now and then we catch the 10:00 news, an educational special on the Public Broadcasting channel, or our once-a-year favorite—the New Year's Day Strauss concert broadcast from Vienna. When our sons were living at home, our oldest son, Chad, probably watched ten hours total in a year. Nate viewed as many sports events as his schedule permitted. Jordan enjoyed watching the *Frugal Gourmet* or any other cooking program, even if it was in a different language! I'm grateful for parents who were protective of my mind when I was young, and I was anxious to pass that favor on to my children. I realize that opinions on television viewing vary greatly from family to family, but listed below are ideas that might stimulate thought and discussion in your home.

Ideas from Other Moms

● For the most part, there is no television viewing in our home from Sunday through Thursday. Instead, we encourage activities, homework, and visiting with each other. We started the children on this track very early, from kindergarten and on through high school. We did make exceptions for certain shows. There are so many more important ways to use our time than on TV viewing. My husband and I lead this by example. (It's easy—we don't like TV anyway!)

● TV has not really been an issue in our house since the boys have reached school age. My sons don't watch TV except for an occasional sporting event because they are so busy with other activities. We have encouraged their involvement in a variety of activities including music lessons, church choirs, Scouts, community theater, weekend classes at local colleges, homework and reading, and several sports. They do not seem to miss TV because they find the other activities challenging, fun, and rewarding.

● When our two oldest children were four and two, we decided to get rid of our television. Now, eighteen years later, we have no regrets. Raising our seven children without the influence of TV was one of the best decisions we ever made. All of the children have been good students and active in sports, music, and church activities. They are good readers, have excellent vocabularies, and are creative in their play. They don't expect to be entertained but make their own fun. Some families may consider total elimination of TV to be a radical move, but it was a great choice for our family.

● When the children were very young, rather than setting a limit or saying no to TV, I filled the home and their schedules with exciting things to do. They figured that if they watched television, they'd miss out on something fun or important. As they have grown older, I have specifically chosen not to watch weekly shows. In other words, I've tried to be a good model for them. It's a great check and balance, and guess what? It works!

● If we have a TV in our home, then we need to have control over it, teach control, and watch it with our kids so we can point out and discuss proper and improper attitudes, life situations, and values. There just isn't that much on TV that's worth watching, so I feel that selected videos, puzzles, games, books, creative play, walks, bike rides, and outdoor play are much better alternatives. It's not just a matter of decreasing television time—we have to fill our time with other activities, so our children will enjoy *not* watching TV.

We have vacillated back and forth on the role of TV in our children's lives and in our own, going from putting the television away to having it around and available. After many years of viewing and reviewing, I think we have decided the less TV, the better. The quality of programs available is getting progressively worse, and there are now programs on during prime time that, in our opinion, should not be viewed by adults, let alone children. A no-TV policy definitely encourages both children and adults to use free time doing constructive things individually and together. One idea that we have tried at different times in our family is to let each child have a certain number of hours per week to watch. They decide at the beginning of the week which programs they wish to watch. When the hours are used up for the week, the TV is turned off.

I remember a time when Judd was about eighteen months old and I rather self-righteously declared to my friend Judy, "I don't use the TV as a baby-sitter." Judy, who by then had four children, laughed and said with love, "Oh, Linda, you're still in that idealistic stage." Anyway, when that "stage" finally passed, a system I used with Judd when he was about three or four, in order to teach him about choices, was to allow him three half-hour programs of television a day (probably too lenient for some people's standards, but I wasn't as idealistic by then, you see). He had to choose those programs from the TV listings ahead of time, rather than just flipping the channels on a remote. Then at the beginning of each week I gave him twenty-one tickets, each one good for one-half hour of viewing. When he would watch those programs, he'd give me a ticket for each half-hour. But the incentive was that if there were any tickets left over at the end of the week, I'd give him ten cents each for those not used. And I usually ended up owing him money.

● TV really robs family time. On the rare occasions when our kids do watch TV, we make it a family time. The program has to be appropriate for everyone watching, and because we're all there together we are sure it is a good choice from start to finish. If we feel uncomfortable with any of the content, we're not afraid to flip it off and do something else. If friends show up, the television goes off.

● We have raised our four children without television, originally because it presented problems for *me* in the area of purity, humor, and time wasted. We purchased a VCR player and a monitor, allowing our kids to watch rented and purchased videos, old musicals, and funny TV reruns.

● One method of regulating TV viewing is the coupon system. An agreed-upon time limit is set for how much TV should be allowed in a week. Half-hour coupons are given to each child for the allotted amount of time, and together with parents, they can choose which programs they want to watch.

● As a mom of several preschoolers, it is tempting to use the TV as a baby-sitter while I get supposedly "more important things" done. Our solution for the past year has been to unplug the antenna and use the television only as a monitor with our VCR. Living close to our church and public libraries, we have access to many free videos for the kids (and ourselves). This allows the timing and selection of material viewed to be more intentional. We've found that we haven't really missed anything, and neither have the kids.

● During the summer when the TV seems to have lots of appeal, we have always said, "You can't watch TV any longer than you read. If you read for a half hour a day, you can watch television for a half hour." They've never tried reading six hours so they could watch TV for six hours!

39

Toddlers

❧

oddlers provide many humorous moments in family living. I remember an amusing incident that happened when Nathan was three. I had just returned home from doing my weekly grocery shopping, and he was helping me unload the bags. Picking up a box of laundry detergent, he took it to the laundry room, came back to the kitchen, and announced with pride, "I put away the washer food for the clothes!" Toddlers observe our routines, even though they don't always understand what's going on.

A toddler is defined as one who walks with short, unsteady steps. Experiencing increasing independence and awareness, toddlers have a deep need for *steadiness* and *stability*. This is the stage of life at which they begin to sense how consistent things are in the home. Will the same behavior on two different days get the same reaction from Mom? Is Mom consistent? If she says no, does she mean it? My personal observations lead me to believe that toddlerhood is the age at which we initially win the respect of our child. Obviously, we continue working at it after the toddler years are past, but I've noticed that moms who can't seem to get respect at that young age have an exceptional challenge when the child hits adolescence.

Keeping our lives simple during the children's toddler years fits in with their ability to handle only small steps. They need lots of repetition and predictability; that's what they thrive on! As I look back on my children's toddler years, there are some things I wish I had done differently, but one thing I'm glad I did was to keep their schedules simple and predictable. We ate at the same times each day. I put them down for naps at the same time each day. I read to them at the same time each day. Bedtime came at the same time each evening. These small routines make things feel secure for the toddler. (Those days are now long gone. My husband and I frequently go to bed *before* our older two children who are up reading for a class, and dinner tonight probably won't happen at the same time we ate last night!) My theory on toddlerhood is that steadiness and simplicity early on promote security that will lead to confidence and flexibility later in life.

Ideas from Other Moms

- When I put my daughter in the stroller to take her shopping or in the car seat on trips, I often tied a small toy to a rubber band and then pinned the rubber band to her bib. I attached several items to keep her busy and happy. She didn't lose the toys, and I wasn't constantly retrieving them.

- When I washed the kitchen floor, I put my daughter in her high chair and taped several pieces of paper to the tray. I also tied two or three crayons to the high chair. Planting the high chair in the next room where she could see me, I was able to wash the floor while she had fun coloring.

- I learned from my oldest that blankets, pacifiers, and other "loveys" can become a problem as the child grows older and is still attached to these items. When my second child came along, I decided he wouldn't be dragging along any of these articles past infancy. He loved his pacifier and a blanket, but both had to stay in the crib when he got out of it. In other words, pacifiers and blankets could be used to comfort when we were rocking before bedtime and while he was in bed, but they were not for any other time. Since that was the rule from early on, it was never a problem.

- Be realistic when you take several young ones out at once. As a mother of twins, I knew my limits where their physical safety might be jeopardized by my lack of hands.

- Start a playgroup of four toddlers. If they play one morning every week, rotate homes so each mother has the group once a month. The moms then have three mornings during the month when they are free to make appointments or have some quiet moments. Set it up like a preschool environment. If the mom in charge spends the morning interacting with, reading to, and playing games with the children, the kids get positive input from another adult, plus they learn to cooperate with their friends.

- Thinking back to potty training days, I found that a simple reward of *one or two* M & M's, depending on you know what, worked quite nicely!

- Being the mom of an active toddler has its ups and downs, but so far I have experienced mostly ups! Reading Dr. James Dobson's book *Dare to Discipline* has helped me put this stage in its proper perspective. Someone told me not to label this stage the "terrible twos," and I thought that was good advice. Instead, I try to think of it as the "independent twos" and keep in mind how important this time is for Brady to learn independence and worth.

● When the children are very little and have colds, I sometimes bring the car seat into the house and put them to sleep in it. Being in an upright position, they don't get as stuffed up, and they sleep better.

● I understand that as a child I was rather precocious, knew no strangers, and always kept my mother on her toes. Well, what goes around, comes around. It is only appropriate that I should have the daughter I have for my youngest. She sat at four months, crawled at six months, walked at nine months, and has never stopped since. She has had an irresistible curiosity since long before she realized it could get her into trouble.

During the summer of 1986 we were on a family vacation that included a day at Greenfield Village near Detroit, Michigan. My daughter was two and a half years old and usually sat in a stroller on family outings. Having decided to shed the stroller for the walk through Daniel Webster's house, we were enjoying moving a little more freely and being a little less conspicuous than usual—until a piercing alarm started ringing. We didn't have to wonder for long what was causing the shrill sound because soon our daughter's cry was accompanying the alarm.

We moved quickly to the source of the tears only to find our daughter's head stuck in the bars dividing the hallway of the home from one of the rooms. We were no longer inconspicuous! As easily as that little head went in through the bars, it refused to come out. It took the combined efforts of the guard, her father, and me to work her head back through to the same side of the bars as her body—with more audience than we cared to have. So much for blending in!

● The old saying, "If he's quiet, he's doing something he's not supposed to" came true for me! I assumed there was nothing my son Christian could get into while I was getting ready to take him to a doctor's appointment. Mind you, this was an appointment we had scheduled a long time in advance with a hard-to-get-in-to-see doctor. All of a sudden, Christian *burst* through the bathroom door and said, "Hi!" He and his primary colored clothes were *white*! He had found the powder bottle and discovered how much fun it was to shake and watch powder poof out of the top. This was one of those days when I had felt pretty relaxed. I hadn't been rushing out the door, Christian was ready, and I thought I had just enough time to get ready without being late. Guess again! Now neither of us was ready. First, I did the really important thing—I took pictures. Then I gave him a bath and cleaned up the puddles of powder he'd left all over the house. It was hard to let my child know that he had done something naughty when it was actually one of the funniest things I had ever seen!

During my pregnancy, I focused my attention on giving birth. I was scared to death about what I would be going through. I worried about how I would know it was time to go to the hospital. I tried to memorize the stages of labor learned in Lamaze. I read my copy of *What to Expect When You're Expecting* every night when I went to bed. I made lists and packed and repacked for the hospital. I spent so much time thinking about the actual labor and delivery that I forgot to think about what would happen once that new life was placed in my arms. No one warned me about the difficulties I would have physically. No one prepared me for all the adjustments I would have to make psychologically.

Once the original excitement of having my son home wore off, the reality of the change started to hit me. It seemed as if nothing but my name was the same. My body was so badly misshapen that I had nothing to wear. My role in life had been permanently changed. I looked in the mirror and did not know the face that gazed back. Everything that I had enjoyed about my life was no longer accessible to me. I couldn't find time to read. I couldn't go to movie theaters.

I didn't seem to have time to see my friends. My husband and I seemed to talk of nothing but our son. I missed my friends at work. I missed the satisfaction and recognition I received from my job. I lost my confidence in myself.

God has really worked on me during this awkward year of my life. He taught me great lessons about where I should be getting my self-esteem. He taught me that it is not what I am doing or how I look that determines who I am. What I am on the inside is what is important. My relationship with Him is the core of everything else I attempt to do in this life. Being obedient to Him and joining Him in His calling is what really matters. Right now, in this season of my life, He has called me to care for one of His precious children.

● Children enjoy their toys more if they have a break from them periodically. I hide a box containing a few of their toys, and every six to eight weeks I make a switch—it's like getting new toys all over again.

● I remember laughing pretty hard when my toddler (who was still potty training) followed me into the bathroom where I was using the toilet and said, "Very *good*, Mommy—you went in the toilet!" We all need words of encouragement from time to time!

● When our oldest son was about two years old, he decided to escape from his grandma who was drying him off after his bath. He ran out the front door and down the street with only his hooded towel flying from his head. Grandma (in her robe!) was in hot pursuit when a car of teenagers drove by and yelled, "Streaker." (Streaking was a big thing in the early seventies.) An embarrassed grandma finally caught her little angel by stepping on the dragging towel and stopping him in his tracks. She hustled him right back home and was not laughing at the time, though since then we've had many chuckles remembering Donnie's escapade!

40

Traditions

~~~❧~~~

Traditions. Every family has them. I remember the excitement I felt as a newlywed, realizing that my husband and I could choose traditions for our own family. We included some from each of our growing-up years and adopted new traditions as well. I baked holly cookies, butterballs, and toffee squares that my mom made every year at Christmas. Jim suggested that we cut down our own Christmas tree like his family had done. We made a new custom of eating at a particularly nice restaurant at the beginning of the new year to discuss the highlights of the previous year.

Some of the traditions we have chosen for our family, such as prayer at mealtime, Bible stories at bedtime for the young ones, and short Bible readings at the breakfast table, have been handed down from our parents. These elements of our life are especially meaningful because they have eternal significance. In God's plan for the world, He has given parents the responsibility of passing truth from one age to the next. "Let each generation tell its children what glorious things [God] does" (Ps. 145:4).

When I asked moms to share their favorite traditions, I received an overwhelming response. Apparently, traditions are important to mothers. I hope some that are included here will warm your hearts!

Ideas from Other Moms

Family Traditions

● During our *long* winters in the Midwest, we anxiously awaited the coming of spring. My children and I baked melt-away cookies, icing them with three or four different pastel colors. Each of my school-aged children took cookies to share with his or her class on the first day of spring.

● Once a month, on the number of the day that is my child's birthday (for example, the 25th if the child's birthday is April 25), I take my child out for lunch or bring a special lunch to school.

● The "Adolescent Trip" described by James Dobson in his ministry has been great for our family. My husband was able to take our son, Mike, away for several days and listen to the tapes on adolescence with him. It was an excellent time of father-and-son bonding with an opportunity to discuss critical topics. I look forward to the same trip with our daughter.

● Pajama rides have been a favorite activity of our family throughout the years. About five minutes after the children are tucked into bed for the night, we blow a train whistle and yell, "Pajama ride, pajama ride!" We all jump into the car with blankets and drive to get a special treat at Dairy Queen, McDonald's, or Taco Bell or pick up some pre-ordered pizza. We sing as we go; we either go through a drive-thru or one person runs in and gets carry-out. The children think it's exciting to be out of the house in their pajamas. We return home and enjoy our treat before tucking them back into bed.

● Our family goes apple picking to an orchard in Wisconsin every fall. Bill and I started going there before we had children, and we figure we have gone there every fall now for twenty years. On the way there, Bill tells the children "how I met your mother in Wisconsin, wooed her, and married her." Once we arrive at the orchard, we pick apples, purchase a pumpkin, Wisconsin cheeses, and summer sausage, eat a picnic lunch, and go antique shopping in town. We top the day off with ice cream cones at our favorite place on the way home.

● My husband and I stay home with our children on New Year's Eve and welcome in the New Year together. Each person in the family chooses the type of fast food they would like for dinner, and we drive around to all of those places (we have seven people in our family, so this takes awhile!). We bring the food back home and pig out. After dinner, we spread our sleeping bags on the family room floor, watch movies, and play games. Whoever is still awake at midnight goes outside to listen to fireworks. Our older kids have actually turned down parties to carry on this tradition!

● I'm keeping a journal of important events in the life of my children, and I plan on presenting it to them at their rehearsal dinner the day before they get married!

● Sometimes traditions have an odd way of getting started! One hot May day I had the swimming pool set up in the back yard when the children came home from school for lunch. I told them they could take off their shoes and socks and wade in it, but they had to wait until after school to swim. They were all wading obediently when the youngest slipped and fell. Of course, he got his clothes wet! The other two scolded, "Oh, are you in trouble!" Having watched from a distance, I ran across the yard, paused, pushed the other two in, and jumped in myself! With all our clothes soaking wet, we laughed and laughed and had a ball. They changed quickly, ate lunch, and got back to school in plenty of time. Now every year in May on the first day of 80 degree weather they run home from school to jump into the pool with their clothes on.

I make birthday banners for our children. Each year I add an item that represents something significant for that year in the child's life. The banner is hung on the front door for the whole month in which the child's birthday falls.

We have a tradition in our family that is called the "ten-year-old dream trip." My husband gets lots of free air miles in business travel each year, and he has decided to use some of them to take each of our children on a dream trip when they turn ten. The only rule is, they have to choose a place within the continental U.S. Our older son, an athlete, chose Cooperstown and the Baseball Hall of Fame. Our daughter, a dancer, chose to go to New York to see a Broadway play and visit Ellis Island. Our nine-year-old son is busy these days poring over maps and discussing all the possibilities for his dream trip with Dad.

At about age six, my son announced that pigs were the most wonderful, intelligent, trainable animals created by God. He did everything he could to convince us of the same thing, and he refused to eat anything made from a pig. My husband found out about Hog Days in Kewanee, Illinois, and has taken him there each Labor Day weekend for many years to celebrate his love of pigs!

I recommend having parents (and grandparents if they are still living) talk on tape about their family history. It is amazing how much we do not know about our parents' childhoods. Having our parents talk, instead of writing, also gives our children insight into their grandparents' personalities and character, should something happen to them while our children are still young and cannot remember them.

When my children were little, we used to celebrate the first day of each season with a special dinner. They made place cards or place mats to illustrate spring, summer, winter, and fall, and I made a dinner that was typical of that time of year. I also gave each person a gift to be used during the season, such as a woolen hat and pair of mittens, bathing suit and sunglasses, or sports equipment. They made a centerpiece or collected flowers. One year for our winter dinner my husband and children made an elaborate snow scene with cotton balls and foil for the frozen pond. I arranged meatballs in the shape of snowmen, with rice for snow around them. If your children like baseball, celebrate spring with a "Take me out to the ball game" dinner—hot dogs, soda, and Cracker Jacks. Then give them a new mitt, tickets to a game, or membership on a team. Many of these things we would do for our children anyway, so it is easy to make it part of the celebration.

Scripture verses focusing on thanks and worship are set out at each person's place at the Thanksgiving table. Before prayer, each one takes a turn reading their verse. This is a great opportunity for everyone to be involved, from a ninety-year-old grandma down to a first-grade beginning reader. We have also put this on video, which is fun to watch later.

Christmas Traditions

Our extended family has a Gingerbread House Party every Christmas season. To make it easy for families to construct a gingerbread house, we glue graham crackers on house-shaped boxes ahead of time. Families are invited to bring candies, cookies, and decorations. Each family works on their house together, and the creations are truly amazing!

- We open most of our gifts to each other on Christmas Day. But each Christmas Eve the girls look forward to opening one gift, which I designate ahead of time. It is always something they can take or wear to bed—perhaps flannel pajamas or a teddy bear—and we open them after the Candlelight Christmas Eve Service at church.

- Several days or even a week before Christmas, we begin opening one present a day. Each present is received with appreciation, and the children are able to better enjoy Christmas Eve as Jesus' birthday and Christmas Day with extended family.

- We like to cut down our own Christmas tree, though sometimes the memory of this is sweeter than actually doing it! We have now cut trees down in nearly every kind of weather, ranging from a -30° windchill to warm, balmy sunshine in the fifties!

- Christmas cards with family pictures are priceless! I've kept a copy of our yearly cards for each of our girls and hope to one day make a scrapbook. It's fun to look back at the pictures over the years.

- I dislike the idea of getting up at dawn on Christmas morning to rush through the opening of gifts, so we have taken a calmer approach! The children sleep until 7:30 or 8:00. They find their stockings and come to our bedroom to show us their loot. Everyone gets "prettied," and then we have a full, cooked breakfast. After the dishes are done and the kitchen is cleaned up, we go to the tree and leisurely open gifts. This makes the morning seem more special.

- I like to make or bake something for our neighbors at Christmastime. (My mom used to bake Swedish Yule bread for our neighbors; then my brother and I delivered the goodies.) I'm not a baker, but I do make English toffee candy, which has now become our tradition. We all make numerous batches, and the girls make the deliveries.

Every year I buy one new ornament for my daughters that is theirs to keep. If we have vacationed at a special place during the year, I try to get an ornament from that location.

My children are nineteen, seventeen, thirteen, and twelve. My oldest child, while still in preschool, made a funny little paper star that has topped our Christmas tree every year. This year I thought he might be embarrassed by it, or that the rest of the kids would be ready for a change. Much to my surprise, but also to my pleasure, they all said Christmas wouldn't be the same without that same little old star adorning the tree. It shone proudly and was a reminder of the needs we all have for tradition and consistency.

Our kids leave Santa pizza and pop just because everyone else leaves him milk and cookies!

Easter Traditions
On the day before Easter, we invite the neighborhood children over for an egg hunt and have them bring their parents to watch and have refreshments in the yard. Each child brings twelve items (bubbles, plastic eggs with Easter candy inside, small prizes, etc.) to our home the day before the hunt. We also ask each family to bring a plate of finger food to share (cookies, fruit, appetizers, donuts, or popcorn). Depending on what the weather is like outside, we serve either hot coffee or iced tea.

Several years ago I came across a meaningful Easter basket tradition that we have used in our family. Having purchased different sized plastic eggs, we number and fill them with the objects and Bible verses listed below. Next, we place them all in a basket. Nine days before Easter my children begin opening them at dinner, one each night. They open the eggs in order of the labeled numbers, with the child who opens the egg also reading the verses inside.

#1—thirty dimes—Matthew 26:14–16.
#2—a piece of bread—Luke 22:14–16, 19–20.
#3—thorns and purple cloth—Mark 15:16–20.
#4—a cross—John 19:16–22.
#5—a nail—Acts 2:22–23.
#6—a strip of cloth or gauze—Matthew 27:57–60.
#7—a smooth stone—Matthew 27:62–66; 28:2–4.
#8—spices or a sachet—Mark 16:1–2.
#9—nothing inside—Luke 24:2–9.

We have made it our family tradition to observe the first Saturday in spring with the festivities that are usually associated with Easter. We don't want our children to confuse the importance of Jesus' death and resurrection with ducks and rabbits. Chickens and bunnies are symbols of spring, so we celebrate the first Saturday of spring with egg hunts and candy-filled baskets. On Easter Sunday we go out to a restaurant for breakfast (to help us set this Sunday apart as special) and then go on to church to praise God for His gift of eternal life.

Notes

1. Alexander MacLaren, *Expositions of Holy Scripture* (Grand Rapids, Mich.: Baker Book House, n.d.), p. 292.

2. Sylvia Rimm, *How to Parent So Children Will Learn* (Watertown, Wisc.: Apple, 1990), pp. 84–85.

3. Walter Wangerin, *As for Me and My House* (Nashville: Thomas Nelson, 1987), pp. 132–33.

4. MacLaren, *Expositions of Holy Scripture*, p. 290.

5. Wangerin, *As for Me and My House*, pp. 60, 63.

6. Matthew Henry, *Matthew Henry's Commentary on the Whole Bible* (Old Tappan, N.J.: Fleming H. Revell, n.d.), pp. 976–77.

7. James Dobson, *Dare to Discipline* (Wheaton, Ill.: Tyndale House, 1970), p. 15.

8. Henry, *Matthew Henry's Commentary on the Whole Bible*, p. 976.

9. Wenham, Motyer, Carson, France, *New Bible Commentary, 21st Century Edition* (Downers Grove, Ill.: InterVarsity Press, 1994), p. 608.

10. Gladys Hunt, *Ms. Means Myself* (Grand Rapids, Mich.: Zondervan, 1972), pp. 22–24.

11. Gladys Hunt, *Honey for a Child's Heart* (Grand Rapids, Mich.: Zondervan, 1969), pp. 17, 21.

12. Charles Bradshaw and Dave Gilbert, *Too Hurried to Love* (Eugene, Ore.: Harvest House, 1991), p. 19.

13. Ibid., p. 24. Emphasis added.

14. Elizabeth A. Carter and Monica McGoldrick, *The Family Life Cycle* (New York: Gardner Press, 1980), p. 296.

15. Frank B. Minirth, M.D., and Paul D. Meier, M.D., *Happiness Is a Choice* (Grand Rapids, Mich.: Baker Book House, 1988), p. 24.

16. Carter and McGoldrick, *The Family Life Cycle*, p. 297.

17. Lee Combrinck-Graham, M.D., *Children in Family Contexts* (New York: Guilford Press, 1989), p. 52.

18. Michael Jaffe, *Understanding Parenting* (Dubuque, Iowa: Wm. C. Brown, 1991), p. 26.

19. Carter and McGoldrick, *The Family Life Cycle*, p. 306.

20. Ibid., p. 14.

21. Dennis and Ruth Gibson, *The Sandwich Years* (Grand Rapids, Mich.: Baker Book House, 1991), p. 17.

22. James S. Hewett, ed., *Illustrations Unlimited* (Wheaton, Ill.: Tyndale House, 1988), p. 498.

23. Dr. Henry Virkler, *Speaking Your Mind Without Stepping on Toes* (Wheaton, Ill.: SP Publications, 1991), p. 132.

24. Brenda Hunter, *In the Company of Women* (Sisters, Ore.: Multnomah, 1994), p. 52.

25. V. Gilbert Beers, *Turn Your Hurts into Healing* (Old Tappan, N.J.: Fleming H. Revell, 1988), p. 30.

26. Rimm, *How to Parent So Children Will Learn*, pp. 96–97.

27. Helen Russ Stough, *A Mother's Year* (Old Tappan, N.J.: Fleming H. Revell, 1905), p. 35.

28. Hewett, ed., *Illustrations Unlimited*, p. 382.

29. Robin Simons, *After the Tears* (Orlando, Fla.: Harcourt Brace Jovanovich, 1987), pp. 34–35.

30. Ibid., p. 36.

31. Ibid., p. 54.

32. Laura Pearlman and Kathleen Anton Scott, *Raising the Handicapped Child* (Englewood Cliffs, N.J.: 1981), p. 27.

33. Simons, *After the Tears*, p. 27.

34. Elinor B. Rosenberg, *The Adoption Life Cycle* (New York: Macmillan, 1992), p. 187.

35. Jodi Scheinfeld, "The Emotional Side of Pregnancy," *Baby on the Way*, Fall 1995, pp. 40–41.

36. "The First Trimester," *Healthy Pregnancy*, Spring 1996, p. 11.

37. Ibid., p. 73.

38. Ibid., p. 44.

39. Fitzhugh Dodson, *How to Single Parent* (New York: Harper and Row, 1987), p. 5.

40. Stough, *A Mother's Year*, p. 95.

Ellen Banks Elwell is a fifty-something mom who enjoys seeing families grow as they practice God's principles for living. A graduate of Moody Bible Institute and American Conservatory of Music, Ellen has written piano arrangements for kids as well as *One Year Devotions for Moms* and *The Christian Grandma's Idea Book*. She makes her home in Wheaton, Illinois, with her husband, Jim, and they enjoy taking beach vacations with their adult children—Chad, Nate and Brit, and Jordan.